INDEPENDENCE TRAINING FOR
VISUALLY HANDICAPPED CHILDREN

CROOM HELM SPECIAL EDUCATION SERIES
Edited by Bill Gillham, Child Development Research Unit,
University of Nottingham

Already Available:

ENCOURAGING LANGUAGE DEVELOPMENT
Phyllis Hastings and Bessie Hayes

INDEPENDENCE TRAINING FOR VISUALLY HANDICAPPED
CHILDREN
Doris W. Tooze

Scheduled for Publication in late 1981:

WORK PREPARATION FOR THE HANDICAPPED
David Hutchinson

TOYS AND PLAY FOR THE HANDICAPPED CHILD
Barbara Riddick

DAILY LIVING WITH THE HANDICAPPED CHILD
Diana Millard

TEACHING POOR READERS IN THE SECONDARY SCHOOL
Christine Cassell

These titles are not all necessarily available in North America from University Park Press

Independence Training for Visually Handicapped Children

DORIS TOOZE

CROOM HELM LONDON

University Park Press • Baltimore

© 1981 Doris Tooze
Croom Helm Ltd, 2-10 St John's Road, London SW11

British Library Cataloguing in Publication Data

Tooze, Doris
    Independence training for visually
    handicapped children.—(Croom Helm special
    education series)
    1. Perceptual — motor learning. 2. Blind-
    Education
    I. Title
    370.15'5   LB1067

    ISBN 0-7099-0290-5

Published in North America by
UNIVERSITY PARK PRESS
300 North Charles Street,
Baltimore, Maryland

ISBN 0-8391-1695-0

Library of Congress Card Number: 81-51003

Printed in Great Britain by Spottiswoode Ballantyne Ltd.,
Colchester and London

Contents

Series Foreword

The Croom Helm Special Education series is explicitly intended to give experienced practitioners in the helping services the opportunity to present a wide range of remedial programmes and techniques which they have developed in practice. The basis of the editorial policy is the belief that there exists much 'good practice' which is almost unknown beyond the local area where it is established or else, as in this instance, widely known but not previously available in book form. The present project is, therefore, concerned with the communication and dissemination of ideas and methods developed by those who use them in their working lives.

Independence Training for Visually Handicapped Children deals with the *joint* role of parents and teachers in helping children with visual impairments to cope independently with the sighted world.

B.G.

Preface

This book is written for the parents and teachers of visually handicapped children. It sets out methods and techniques of mobility training which, if gradually absorbed by a child as a way of living, will enable him to become truly independent.

This book could not have been written without the help of many people: firstly my husband, Freddie Tooze, who as headmaster of Tapton Mount School made independence part of the ethos of the school. He has further helped me with advice and encouragement in the writing of the book. I should like to thank all the children and parents who have joined me in the development of mobility training over the years and who have added to my knowledge of the subject. I am indebted to many colleagues and would like to name two: Romayne Gayton for her helpful advice in the chapter dealing with young children and _June Lamyman_ whose methods of teaching, eating and dressing are described in the same chapter. I should also like to thank David and Janet Weaver and Eamon and Maureen Preston for allowing us into their homes to photograph their children and Sam Grainger of the University of Nottingham for his excellent photography throughout the book. Finally I am very grateful to the series editor, Bill Gillham, for his help and for giving me the opportunity of putting my ideas into print.

D.T.

CHAPTER 1

Essential Factors for Independence

Those who have not had the experience of having a handicapped child cannot really appreciate the feelings of parents who find themselves in this situation. Parents come to terms with the problem in different ways. In many cases where the child is visually handicapped, they resolve to compensate for their child's handicap by 'being his eyes' and doing everything for him. This understandable response is, in fact, the worst solution that they could adopt. It leads to the child becoming completely dependent on his family. A dependent child will be a dependent adult and as such will be unable to achieve his true potential. Such an adult is likely either 'to have a chip on his shoulder' or 'to retreat into his shell', depending on the personality of the individual. Nobody can be another person's eyes; real experience must come from the individual himself, and the visually handicapped child must come to appreciate his world through active experience using his other senses and any residual vision he may have.

Prospects for the visually handicapped person today are better than they have ever been. There are a multiplicity of aids available, including electronic devices, which can help him to take a fuller and more active part in society. Closed-circuit television equipment enables a person with very limited vision to read print. American researchers have produced a machine that can translate print symbols which can be read by touch and so interpreted by a totally blind person. This machine — the Optacon — is now being used in Western countries by those working in commerce. Children attending schools for the visually handicapped are now being taught to read by this method, as well as by the more conventional Braille alphabet. The versatility of the Optacon is being extended by the use of a computer to translate the print symbols into speech. Although the market price of this machine renders it unrealistic at the moment, there is no doubt that in the future it will become more generally available. There are also 'talking calculators' and many types of obstacle detector on the market.

However, aids by themselves will be of little use in integrating a visually handicapped person into society unless the person himself is socially acceptable. He must be able to interact within his community, not as an object of pity, constantly dependent on the goodwill of others, but as a person of equal standing. Independence is the key to acceptance.

Essential factors for independence are *orientation, mobility* and *daily living skills.* Parents can ensure that their handicapped child will be able to achieve true independence if they themselves learn to understand these skills and are prepared to give early training in them to their children.

Orientation

Orientation is the ability to understand the relationship that objects have to one another — the creation of a mental pattern of the environment. But it is more than this, for having perceived the pattern, the subject must then be able to put himself into it: to relate it to his own position and movements. This is very difficult for the congenitally blind, i.e. those who have never had any sight from birth. For these children an early start to training is essential.

The first step in orientation is the achievement of an awareness of one's own body and the relationship of the different parts of the body to each other. Furthermore, a blind person will need to rely on the position of his own body to other objects about him in order to place himself in space. He needs therefore to be aware of his left and right side. Sighted people tend to laugh at their inability to judge right from left; this for them is of minor importance — except when they are driving a car! However, for a blind child who will constantly be assessing his position in space from touching objects or being aware on which side of his body objects lie, it is of great importance.

Sensory Development Necessary for Achieving Orientation

It is impossible for a person without sight to orientate himself in space without the extended use of his other senses of which *hearing* provides the major compensation. With this sense, clues may be picked up at a distance. For example, the constant relationship between the three sounds, the ticking of the clock on the wall, the low buzz of the refrigerator and the sound of the birds singing outside, provide a pattern that enables me to fix my position in my kitchen without using my sight. Similarly, the sound of traffic will allow a blind pedestrian to perceive the line of the road he is walking along, and he may be aware of the proximity of a side road from the sound of a car changing gear preparatory to entering or leaving the main road.

The above are all examples of direct sound. Indirect sound is sound which having been emitted from one source bounces back to the listener off an obstacle thus making an echo. The skill of using such echoes to orientate oneself is called *echo location*. The blind pedestrian can easily learn to tell the difference in the echo sound of his footsteps when walking through a narrow passageway or tunnel from the echoes of his footsteps at the point where the path widens or the tunnel ends. Another example of the value of noting a change in echo sound is experienced if, when standing behind a bus shelter, he listens to passing cars. Two note changes can be identified as each car passes first one end and then the other end of the shelter; these sounds will allow a blind person to 'place' the shelter. By constant listening for such changes of sound, blind people improve their auditory skill in the higher frequencies; they are then able to appreciate the slight changes of sound as they pass gateways, posts, shop entrances, etc. and so locate themselves more accurately within the environment.

The *haptic sense* which is the sense of touch is another channel of information for the visually handicapped person through which his environment can be revealed. This sense can be divided into two parts: *tactile discrimination* and *manual dexterity*. It is the former aspect that comes into play for orientation purposes. Manual dexterity is needed for daily living skills and will be discussed in a later section.

The sense of touch is often associated with the hands in the same way that the sense of taste is associated with the tongue and the sense of hearing with the ears. In fact, unlike the other senses where the necessary sensory receptors are situated in one specific part of the body, the sensory receptors responsible for touch are situated under the skin of the whole area of the body. In orienting himself a blind person will therefore be able to use the most convenient part of his body for touch purposes: such as the backs of his heels to ensure he is square to a wall preparatory to walking to the other side of a room, or the back of his hand to check that he is walking parallel to a wall.

For distinguishing fine detail bare skin is by far the most efficient, and indeed the skin that has not acquired a hardened layer is the most receptive. For this reason Braille is more easily learnt by young children whose fingers are still soft than by elderly people whose hands are hardened. Similarly, a mother will often test her baby's bath water with her elbow rather than her hand. Minute differences of ground surface are easily perceived when one is walking barefoot and blind children should be encouraged to walk barefoot in the house and garden to become aware of such differences. None the less impressions can be obtained through touch when the skin is hardened, or when it is covered, and even when the impressions come from an implement which is held in the hand such as a long cane. Such impressions are sufficiently effective to act as clues in orientation. Fine detail is not always required for identification of objects and if it is, further investigation can be carried out with the hands once an object has been located.

The *olfactory sense* which is the sense of smell is obviously useful to the blind person in providing environmental clues that, for example, enable him to locate shops. People are aware of fish shops and bakeries by their smell but many other areas have a unique odour which will reinforce a blind person's knowledge of where he is. Thus the fumes from a petrol pump may well remind a blind pedestrian that the driveway he is crossing belongs to a garage; he can expect another entrance or exit driveway almost immediately, and so he must be on the alert for cars.

The *kinaesthetic sense* is concerned with movement and is controlled by the neuro-muscular system of the body. A person with a good kinaesthetic sense is likely to enjoy physical exercise, have a good rhythm in movement and, because of the natural ability to co-ordinate his limbs, he will be able to acquire easily a good posture and gait. A young blind child with a naturally good kinaesthetic sense will continue to explore his environment in spite of any bumps that he may encounter.

The kinaesthetic sense is also responsible for 'muscular memory'. This is the ability to repeat actions without conscious thought once they have been learnt. These actions extend from simple movements such as walking, skipping, cycle riding and so on, to quite complicated travel routes that a person may take such as the route from his home to his place of work. Any action, if repeated often enough, can be committed to 'muscular memory' but the time taken to learn it can be considerably reduced if the other senses are brought into play to help in the learning process. Sighted people make use of landmarks to help them fix a route in their memory; visually handicapped people need to use their other senses for this purpose. It requires much practice and parents themselves need to be aware of non-sighted clues in order to be able to point them out to their children. The fact that so much of our movement in familiar places, such as the home, is learnt by constant repetition may also mask the fact to parents that their child needs this training, constantly and systematically.

Residual Vision

Sight plays an important role in co-ordinating impressions obtained from the other senses. This function enables a person to judge the size and shape of objects, their composition, weight and surface texture, the distance they are from him and the distance between one object and another. Where a visually handicapped child has some residual vision, this should be developed to the full so that the co-ordinating function of sight may be maximised as far as possible. It should be noted that the majority of visually handicapped children do indeed possess some useful residual vision; research in several countries has indicated that the proportion may well be as high as 80 per cent.*

It should not be assumed therefore, that because a child is visually handicapped the use of sight should be ignored. Ophthalmologists cannot always tell how much sight a small child has, nor how effectively the child uses it. Training in the use of residual vision is a very important part of the remedial work in schools for the visually handicapped. Its importance in developing a sense of orientation cannot be over-emphasised. A child who can tell the difference between light and dark will at least be able to locate the window side of a room. There are some people who have sufficient vision to enable them to be aware of an obstacle in their path although

---

* Kaplan, USSR, 1966. 80% of blind school population with some degree of potentially useful vision.
Kederis and Ashcroft, USA, 1970. 79% of legally blind children with useful residual vision.
CTB Report to Vernon Committee, UK, 1969. 77% of blind school population with visual acuity of 2/60 Snellen and upwards.

they are unable to perceive an accurate outline of it; this is called *shadow vision*. Such stimuli can be used to help a person steer a clear path. With higher visual acuity, children can be trained to recognise objects by their shape or by other distinguishing characteristics, as in the case of a pillar box or telephone kiosk.

Partially-sighted people need to know the cause of their eye defect and the effect it has on their vision. People suffering from the eye defect *retinitus pigmentosa,* for example, are likely to suffer from 'night blindness'; this means that although they have good mobility during the day when the light is good, they are unable to see as well when it gets dark so will then need a long cane to detect 'down kerbs'.

Map Making

Map making and the use of maps to follow routes are two activites that form an important part of orientation training. By this means the lay-out of the environment can be contracted to a representation small enough to be felt within the span of the hands. Thus a blind person is enabled to appreciate the pattern of his immediate environment and the relationship between different objects within it. Each child should make his representation rather than following one that has been made for him. These representations can begin with the simple practice of arranging furniture in a 'Wendy House' to simulate the lay-out of the furniture of a known room, to the more sophisticated raised line map of the neighbourhood, including familiar shops, the local park and so on (see Chapter 6).

Mobility

Mobility training involves the acquisition of the set of skills and techniques which enable a visually handicapped person to travel more easily through his environment. These skills cover a wide spectrum of activities. They are first seen in the 'toddler' learning how to find his way around his own house, and range to the travel techniques which eventually enable the adult to travel the world independently. Chapter 5 will deal more fully with mobility training; here the main mobility aids are described.

Mobility Aids

The use of aids forms an integral part of mobility training. The most widely used aid is, strangely enough, a *sighted person*. A blind individual, well trained in mobility, will be able to use a sighted person as a guide fairly readily and, more important still, he can do this without losing his independence. He can get help from a member of the general public when the situation requires it, and can relinquish it again when assistance is no longer needed.

The use of sticks or *canes* to help the blind to make their way about is as old as the affliction itself, although there is now a greater diversity of canes and different methods of using them. The short cane (or medium cane) for instance, proves to be more useful to those people with good residual vision and its use is described in the mobility scheme for the partially sighted (see p. 100). The use of the long cane is the aid best suited to the training of children with no sight or those whose sight is very poor. The cane is an obstacle detector; it detects 'down kerbs' and 'up kerbs' but must be used in such a way that while it is of benefit to its user it is not a danger to other pedestrians. The foremost advantage in teaching this method of travel to blind children is that they acquire a true understanding of their environment as they come increasingly to rely on themselves, the cane being only an extension of the

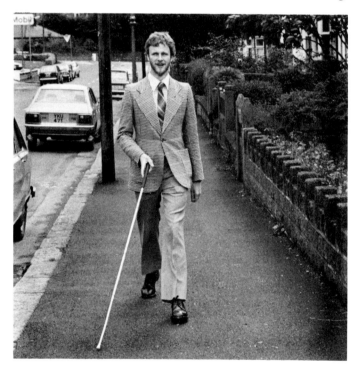

arm. The long cane is also a useful aid for adults. It is cheap, and a folding cane is available which is less cumbersome to carry when not in use than a rigid one.

The *guide dog* is a traditional aid to mobility particularly for the adult blind. Even with this aid the blind person must still be able to orientate himself within his environment for he needs to instruct the dog concerning the route to be taken. However, the dog does take some of the strain out of travel for it will become responsible for the avoidance of obstacles and the anticipation of kerbs, and

moreover, be a companion for whom the owner must care. This means that the blind person must feed and exercise the dog and consequently will exercise himself.

Sonic aids are a great asset in echo location, particularly for the adventitiously blind, i.e. those who were not born blind and consequently may not have developed their hearing to the extent that the congenitally blind have done. The principle of the aid is that a high frequency sound is projected on to any obstacle within its range; the echoes received back from the obstacle allow the user to take avoiding action. The echo pattern changes as the user gets nearer which allows him to judge the distance between himself and the obstacle.

The majority of the aids available are used as adjuncts to the cane. The Kay Torch and the Mowat Vibrator are both hand-held; the latter aid provides

information by 'vibrations' which increase in speed as the user approaches the obstacle. This makes an alternative to sound and is especially liked by children. It is also useful to the hard of hearing. A development of the Kay Torch is the Sonic Glasses, where the emitting and receptor cells are fitted into spectacle frames and worn on the face. These identify overhead obstacles and at the same time the wearer uses a long cane to give him a clear path at ground level (see illustration). The latest sonic aid to be marketed is the Laser Cane. This has three beams which identify objects at three levels: each level has its own different tone.

Many young blind people prefer to use their own hearing and it is good for them to develop their natural abilities. Nevertheless, some experience in the use of sonic aids will be of value to them. There are, for example, occasions when the hand-held aids are very useful, as when trying to locate a pedestrian crossing post in a road where heavy traffic drowns sound, or in following a companion into a restaurant. Before the ability to use any aid is mastered, however, it may well seem to be a hindrance rather than a help. A clear example of this is when children are being taught to come downstairs using a long cane. A start is made on stairs which they use everyday and where they would not normally require an aid; this allows them to concentrate on the correct positioning of the cane. Nearly all children become tense

and stiff on this first occasion in spite of the familiarity of the stairway, but as soon as the lesson is over and the cane dispensed with they come down effortlessly! Once they have learnt the cane technique, however, they are able to negotiate stairs and steps in unfamiliar surroundings as easily as they do the stairs in their own homes.

The more experience of the different aids that can be given to blind people, the greater the choice of options will be and the better travellers they will become. Different aids suit different individuals and in different situations; it is only by personal experience that a blind person will be able to make his choice from the wide range of aids available today.

Daily Living Skills

Daily living skills are the skills that govern how we conduct ourselves in our everyday lives, and include personal hygiene, how we stand and walk, sitting positions, how we eat and, most importantly, how we interact with other people. These skills are not inherent in us but are determined by the culture of the country in which we live, our sex and our time. In India, for example, one may sit cross-legged on the floor, but it is important that the back is straight and the head held correctly. One may eat food with the fingers but again one must eat correctly using the forefinger and thumb to touch the food, not so easy as it sounds! In America, a knife is used to cut all the meat up on the plate; then the fork is transferred to the right hand and used by itself. In France it is acceptable to use bread as an aid to push food on to the fork, and so on. How we sit in our country depends on our sex. A male may sit in a chair with his legs stretched forward and apart; a female must keep her legs together and bent at the knees. This is course connected with the way we dress.

   Much of our knowledge of daily living skills is gained through imitation and in many cases is unconscious. A baby will hold his spoon in the 'grab position' which is the only one he can manage at first. The change to a 'pen-holder' grip is usually initiated by his noticing that his parents hold their spoons in a different way, which he then copies. In our interactions with other people, sight plays a large part. 'Eye-to-eye' contact enables a person within a group to know when it is his turn to speak — and when his audience has had enough of his speech! A visually handicapped person is disadvantaged in this respect but he can be taught the basic rules of conversational give-and-take and, through hearing, he can learn to react to the slight inflections of voice when his listeners reply.

   There are therefore two distinct areas of teaching necessary for a visually handicapped child. He must know how to *interact,* involving behaviour that he would normally gain through sight, and he will need help in acquiring necessary living skills. This help may have to continue into late childhood as some skills are more difficult to master without sight. Walking is a good example of this; all parents spend a lot of time teaching their babies to walk. Walking depends on the ability to balance correctly and for this reason a baby's first steps will be taken with the feet slightly apart and his weight well back which gives him a more stable balance. Once he has perfected this baby walk, parents do not need to teach further. As muscular co-ordination develops his balance will improve; he will unconsciously start to transfer his weight from the back foot before the front foot touches the ground. Balance without sight is far more difficult and the totally blind child is likely to retain his 'baby walk' by not transferring the weight from the back foot before the front foot has explored the ground in front. This prevents him from having too many bumps. As he is unaware that he is walking any differently to anyone else and the walk suits his needs, he is unlikely to change unless encouraged to do so. Parents may think it is not important that their child has a rather peculiar gait, but walking is a habit and it is very difficult to change the style later on. What is acceptable in a child is not so acceptable in an adult, so early and continuing teaching is important. It is interesting to note that if a child loses his sight after he has learnt to walk he does not regress but keeps a correct transference of weight.

Other Factors

The acquisition of skills needed for independence is not easy and requires a good deal of drive and persistence on the part of the visually handicapped child. How independent a child becomes depends on several factors: personality, motivation and the pattern of behaviour expected of him by his family. One cannot expect a young child to be self-motivated towards independence as it is so much easier for him to have everything done for him. If he constantly hears his brothers and sisters being told that they must fetch and carry for him because he cannot see, he is likely to accept the situation and use it to his advantage. Parents may feel that making a handicapped child do things for himself will cause other people to think they are uncaring in their attitude. This may be reinforced by neighbours who tend to become sentimental when they encounter a blind child. But in many ways it is much easier and quicker for the parents to do everything for the child; he will accept this and will be 'less trouble'. Yet true caring is provided by parents who can look ahead for their child and make his world real for him and so fit him for a meaningful life.

The position in the family of the handicapped child in relation to his brothers and sisters needs to be considered. Family life cannot be centred around one of them without creating resentment in the others. Each child in the family has his own rights and needs, and although the handicapped child may require extra help from everyone, he must also learn to give as well as to take. If taken in a balanced perspective, unfolding to a blind child the world around him through developing his other senses can be rewarding for all members of a family; the joint responsibility for helping the handicapped person towards independence can have a unifying influence which actually enhances family life.

CHAPTER 2

Becoming Aware of the Environment

My husband, for many years headmaster of Tapton Mount School for the Visually Handicapped in Sheffield, used to say that the aim of our school was to make each child curious. This is an excellent maxim for parents of visually handicapped babies. Unless actively stimulated, a blind baby will not explore his world fully but will probably remain passive, continuing to take an interest in his own body only, when normal babies of a similar age have progressed to investigating things about them that have caught their eye. This passive attitude can make life seemingly much easier for a busy mother who will know that if she puts her blind baby down he is likely to remain there. A visually handicapped mother once complained to me that her second child, who was fully sighted, was much harder to look after than Valerie her elder daughter who was totally blind. 'Valerie', she said, 'was a good baby. I could put her down anywhere and know that she could stay put; whereas Shirley is into everything and I am worn out with watching her!' Although one must feel sympathetic towards a mother who has a visual handicap herself, there was no doubt that the 'good' blind baby had not had the same opportunities of discovery as her 'naughty' sister.

The aim of this chapter is to suggest 'opportunities for discovery', ways of stimulating curiosity in the young visually handicapped child and thereby encouraging the development of motor skills in an active exploration of his environment.

Acquiring Listening Skills

Sound must replace sight as the stimulating sense that excites exploration, particularly for those babies who are totally blind. Parents need to be aware, themselves, of the information that can be gained from sound when sight is excluded. First they will need to blindfold themselves. Blindfolds can be made from any dark material folded over with the ends joined by a piece of elastic. Alternatively, 'sleep shades' can be bought from a chemist's. Whatever is worn must prevent *any* use of vision; it is often necessary to line the blindfold with a tissue as the bridge of the nose may cause a gap admitting light. Before the parents walk about the house blindfolded, they have to learn the technique of 'arm protection'.

This technique is one of the mobility skills and is set out in Chapter 5. By learning and using it themselves, parents will realise its value and will later be able to teach it to their child.

Practice under the blindfold can become more fun if both parents participate, each taking a turn. In outlining these practice activities, the parent under the blindfold will be labelled *A* and the partner *B,* for the sake of clarity. First parent *A* should sit in the living room and listen to the sounds that he/she can hear and try to identify them. Some sounds are continuous like the sound of the clock ticking. Other sounds are intermittent like those that come from outside the house which will locate the windows, or the sounds coming from another room that may locate a wall or an open doorway. Partner *B* should then turn on the radio or television to show how a loud noise will drown all other sounds. The sound of *B* moving about the room will assist *A* in the perception of space. *B* should continue to walk about the room either rattling keys or keeping up a conversation and *A* should point to him as he moves. When *B* finally comes towards *A,* the latter should call out 'Stop!' when he thinks *B* is within touching range.

A more difficult extension to this exercise is to have *B* walk to the door and for *A* to call 'Stop!' when he thinks *B* has reached it. *A* will probably find that he is judging by time rather than by sound; distance is very difficult to judge without sight, but the combination of sound and time can enable a blind person to make some distance judgements.

When both parents have tried the above listening exercises, *A* should try moving towards one of the sound clues he hears in the room that helped him to locate a particular object. If there is a clock on the mantlepiece that *A* can hear ticking, for example, he should get up and go towards it. (It is a good idea to make sure that the fire is turned off or guarded first!) *A* should become aware of the ticking getting louder as he comes nearer to the clock; when he thinks he is within touching range he should stop. If *A* then turns his head from side to side, he can adjust his position until he thinks he is exactly in line with the clock. To test this he should first touch his nose with his hand and then reach forward to touch the clock. Although *A* may be in line with the clock, if he has approached it from an angle he will not be in line with the mantlepiece but by placing both hands on the shelf he can adjust his position and 'square up' with it (see Chapter 5). From this position, *A* should turn so that his back is square to the mantlepiece, listen to another sound clue and repeat the exercise.

If parents find that there are a lack of sound clues in the room, an RNIB Sound Beacon (see illustration) may be used for these activities. The Sound Beacon emits three different sounds by the movement of a switch. It will also be found useful for a variety of games that can be played with children and which will be referred to in this book as they become relevant.

When parents have become accustomed to moving around in a room they can extend their 'blindfold walking' throughout the rest of the house. Later on they can do exercises within the neighbourhood by using the sighted guide method of travel

(see illustration and p.70 for details of the basic grip). If parents wish to walk only for a short time without sight, they can simply close their eyes — as long as they keep

the sighted guide hold with their partner. By this means they will learn to appreciate the non-sighted clues that are available in the neighbourhood. Many people find that once sight is excluded they become more aware of gradients, sounds and smells.

Some parents of older children have increased their own skill in blind travel by taking lessons using the 'Long Cane' either from a Mobility Officer or from the Mobility Teacher at the school their child attends. These parents have found it helpful to have done some 'Long Cane' training for two reasons: first, it has made them more confident in their child's ability to travel alone and secondly, it has been beneficial in showing them the most useful clues to point out to their son or daughter when going along a new route.

Parents who have experienced some of the above activities will have learnt to appreciate that there are a lot of sounds around them of which they have not previously been aware simply because they were not listening for them. One of the myths about blind people is that they are compensated for their lack of sight by having more acute hearing, an extra gift. This is not true; but their hearing will *become* more acute through use. Parents can encourage their children to increase their listening skills; in time they will be able to use this enhanced hearing for orientation purposes.

Using Music and Meaningful Sounds

If they are to learn to listen, children need good listening conditions. Continual background music in a home is no help to a visually handicapped child. Music at specific times, however, is a great asset; it encourages movement and rhythm in a child. Parents should dance with their child at first to show him how to move. If they just leave him listening to records without this teaching, the child is likely to react with a typical 'blind mannerism': his movement consisting of vigorous rocking in time to the music usually with his finger or fist in his eye. But young children, if played with, quickly react to music with rhythmic and varied movements.

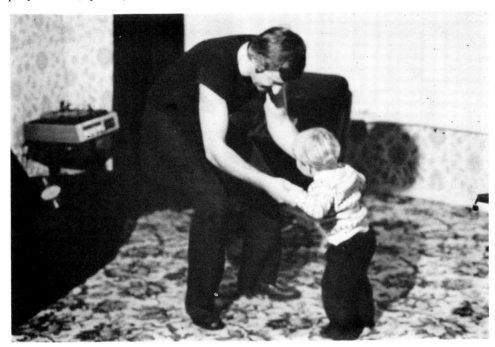

Some parents tape-record jingles and nursery rhymes and their children have favourites for which they ask. Children will also move to other types of music. The little boy in the illustration likes to dance to Irish jigs, for example, and some children enjoy moving to the beat of pop music. Perhaps the best introduction of all to music and movement is for the parents to sing to their child. A useful book to buy which has varied rhymes and jingles in it is *This Little Puffin Nursery Songs and Rhymes,* published by Penguin Books. There are also some very good television and radio programmes for the under-fives in which both mother and child can participate and as these programmes are broadcast at regular times each day, they create a listening routine for a child as well as giving him a great deal of pleasure. 'Listen with Mother' is an example of a particularly well-loved radio programme in the UK.

Noise must be meaningful to a blind child; it is no use being able to hear a noise if the child cannot identify it. One mother made a point of shaking her baby's bottle as she approached him with it and he reacted to the *sound* of the bottle in the same way that a sighted baby reacts to the sight of his bottle. One way of introducing a young baby to household noises and, incidentally, to household smells is for his mother to have him strapped to her back when she is doing some of her household chores. There is a variety of baby carriers on the market that can be used for this purpose. It is advisable to buy a good one with a headrest; they are also useful when taking a baby shopping. If she carries her baby as she works about the house, it is a good plan for the mother to verbalise her actions. For example, the opening of a drawer, the sound of putting in cutlery and the closing of the drawer make three distinct sounds which can be talked through and may give valuable sound training even if the baby is still at the pre-language stage. Some paediatricians believe that all babies benefit by being carried around in this fashion; it is certainly invaluable for visually handicapped babies.

Most people have had the unpleasant experience of being startled by a person suddenly speaking when they have been unaware of his approach. A visually handicapped baby is very much at risk in this respect. To avoid this, a baby should be spoken to from the moment anyone enters the room. This not only prevents the baby from being startled but also allows him to obtain some conception of space. Piaget, the Swiss child psychologist, maintained that a child's first conception of space comes from watching his mother move about the room; in this way the concept of 'near and far' becomes established. The sound of his mother's voice coming towards him and then receding can help a blind child to establish this concept. Other basic concepts can also be appreciated by playing 'Hunt the Beacon'. This game is played in the same way as the old game of 'Hunt the Thimble'. The RNIB beacon is switched on and hidden and then has to be found. The concepts of 'under and over', 'behind and in front' and 'high and low' can be taught and appreciated. The game may also give mothers an opportunity to talk about the limitations of sight. Mothers can explain that when an object is under something, just as hands cannot feel it, neither can eyes see it. Blind children sometimes expect their mother to be able to retrieve dropped toys immediately which may have rolled out of her sight.

Listening times should be an important part of a blind child's upbringing and can begin when he is just a tiny baby. Parents can listen with their baby to the sounds within the environment. These can be: nature sounds such as the birds singing or the wind blowing; household sounds like the ticking clock or the hum of the refrigerator; the road sounds of cars and lorries. Although for very young babies the sound of traffic should not be too near, it is pleasant for them to listen to passing cars from a window inside the house. If parents become interested in sounds they will find examples for themselves. A teacher at Tapton Mount School for the Visually Handicapped collected thirty-five articles each making a different sound and she was able to introduce different activites with them. For example, the children divided them into pleasant and unpleasant sounds; some of the articles she hung up in her classroom as mobiles. One of the children in the class told me she had a mobile hanging near the window in her bedroom which tinkled when the window was open.

Body Awareness and Motor Development

Handling and Play

A blind child must be well aware of the different parts of his body to position himself in space. The best way to learn 'body awareness' is through play. Every baby thrives on the loving handling he gets from his mother and a blind baby is particularly in need of this form of play. Naming and stroking the parts of the body as he is dried after a bath, playing such games as 'This little piggy went to market' and 'Round and round the garden went the teddy bear', all make a baby aware of his body. Awareness of his front and back are experienced on mother's knee or on a flat padded table if she uses one to change his nappy; and the action of rolling over will

be enjoyed if incorporated into a play activity. Every baby enjoys movement and likes his pram to be rocked or to ride in cars, but it is more important to feel the movement directly on his own body when his parents rock him, roll him and when father swings him up above his head.

Continual naming of the baby's sides from an early age will help to give the child a left-right awareness. A game that had significance for one blind child was played sitting on his mother's knee. His mother would say, 'Where's your nose?' and the child would touch his own nose; 'Where is Mummy's nose?' and the child would touch her nose, and so on. The game continued with different parts of the body. By this means the child learnt not only the major parts of his body, but also the less obvious parts such as knuckles, elbows and cheeks.

The floor is a most important place for babies and young children. Babies learn body awareness through relating their bodies to the floor and later, parents can help this process of relationship by active play on the floor with their children.

When introducing a visually handicapped baby to the floor as a play area, his spatial concept of the room can be enlarged by playing in different parts of the room on successive occasions. The baby will become aware of the features of the room and the way in which these features relate to him and to each other. By the fireside (well guarded, of course), he will feel the warmth on his side; similarly, if another time he is placed under a window he will hear the outside sounds at his back. Some parents feel that it is unnecessary to make their child aware through sound and touch of different parts of the room as the child will soon learn to move where he wants without these clues. This is certainly the case in the child's own home where movement patterns are built up through neuromuscular memory and unconscious absorption of clues. However, later on, the child will be required to move in unfamiliar rooms where the concept of a whole will be a necessity. A sighted child acquires this concept through sight at an early age, but a congenitally blind child needs a lot of help to appreciate the concept of wholeness through his other senses. If, from being very young, he has been used to relating himself to the available clues to be found in any room he will later be able to orientate himself more easily in unfamiliar rooms.

A young child who has had experience of rough play with his father will start to initiate movements for himself. Relationships between the floor and his body are felt in such movements as rolling; here the movement may be started with the whole of the back in contact with the floor, then the left side, followed by the front and then with the back once again. The movement can continue until stopped by an obstacle and then repeated the opposite way. Somersaults are another example of a movement where the body comes in contact with the floor in sequence. Most children enjoy doing somersaults, although they need quite a lot of help at first to ensure that the head is kept clear of the ground. Crawling is another physical activity that relates the limbs to the floor in a moving pattern. It is not a necessary stage of walking; many blind children do not crawl before they walk. A sighted child usually crawls in order to get something that has 'caught his eye' during the pre-walking stage. It is, however, an excellent activity for blind children to learn as the movement of the arms in opposition to the legs counterbalances an otherwise excessive rotation of the hips. For this reason it may help to give a blind child a good gait. A game that young children enjoy which involves crawling is as follows. Parent and child both chant the jingle:

Tommy went into the jungle,
Tommy went into the jungle,
Tommy went into the jungle,
And what did Tommy see? . . .

The child or parent then chooses an animal and both crawl about the room with accompanying noises. If there are other members of the family to join in it is even more fun!

Climbing and Balancing

As a baby grows his play becomes more active and the play area is no longer one part of the room but the whole room. The custom in modern homes of having a dining area in the kitchen thus leaving the sitting room less crowded is excellent for blind youngsters. A toddler who has low soft furniture to climb and bounce on is lucky indeed. It may not be so good for the furniture but it is excellent for mobility.

Blind children love climbing and feel safer with this form of activity than just moving in an empty space. Especially enjoyable is the climbing activity that leads to a reward! The little boy in the illustration actually climbs up on to the sideboard

using the drawer handles as steps; this enables him to play with the interesting objects he finds on top.

Through climbing activities, a blind child can become aware of himself in relation to objects, and understand the relationship of one object to another. For example, the action sequence below shows a child who is not only enjoying a play in the bathroom but is incidentally learning the relationship of the bath to the lavatory, and the lavatory and bath to the windowsill.

Standing and walking alone will probably take a longer time to acquire for a totally blind child than for a sighted one; as was pointed out in the first chapter, standing and walking are dependent on balance. Low furniture is a boon to a child wanting to try out his legs with good support. Babywalkers have proved useful and enjoyable for some toddlers. Trucks and push-toys are also helpful in maintaining balance and, additionally, such apparatus also takes the first bumps! The child in the accompanying illustrations finds his 'lion on wheels' useful for this purpose both inside and outside the house.

The main reason for the peculiar gait which tends to be characteristic of those who are born without sight, is poor balance. It is the difficulty of balance that causes the child to keep his body tilted backwards and bend his knees so lowering the centre of gravity. This induces a late transference of weight. A game to play that will increase the sense of balance and encourage the use of reflexes which maintain balance is as follows. Balance is more difficult to maintain as the base decreases so the game is started with a broad base. To obtain this, the child must have not only his feet on his floor but the knees and hands as well. He should then pick up one limb at a time, so leaving three limbs on the ground. The game continues with his keeping only two limbs on the ground and he can be encouraged to try different combinations of limbs. Finally, the child practises standing on one leg, first holding on to an object for support, then without support. It is also stimulating to move in any of the above positions, forward, backward or even sideways.

Another excellent activity to improve balance is for a child to walk along the top of a small wall with his hand being held by an adult. The height raises the centre of gravity so the child is able to obtain an exhilarating feeling of being a little unstable but quite safe as he is holding his parent's hand.

Measuring one's height on a wall encourages a child to stretch to his full extent. Some parents mark their child's height on the wall and so keep a record. To make the marks meaningful to a visually handicapped child, shiny, sticky tape can be used.

Fear prevents a good gait; each step that one takes with a normal walk puts one momentarily off balance. Pushing trucks and other toys, as mentioned above, is a great confidence-builder and encourages weight transference. Learning to jump from a low height also gives a child confidence. Some children are naturally less fearful and will launch themselves forward into space to be caught by their father; others are very timid and need plenty of encouragement. They should never be forced to jump alone or pulled forward from a height. Many blind children like to go through the intermediary stages. First a grown-up should hold them firmly round the waist. When helping a child to jump this way the grown-up should get the rhythm of the jump into his voice, 'and . . .*up!*'; the 'and' should be accompanied by a gentle pull down so that the child bends his knees in preparation for the jump. The 'up' should be accompanied with a good upward thrust. The next stage is to hold both hands, following this by holding one hand, and finally a timid child may need the comfort of only one finger until he reaches the stage of wanting to jump alone.

A congenitally blind child will probably need help in learning to jump from foot to foot. Without this teaching he may always jump on the spot with both feet together. Such a child tends to keep to this way of jumping as it affords him a broader base, and as he cannot see to imitate, he continues to jump in the way he feels secure. The ability to transfer body weight from foot to foot comes into many aspects of movement, in particular dance activities. The child will need specific teaching in changing his weight from one foot to the other. Blind children who have not received such help tend very noticeably — because very oddly — to bounce on the spot off two feet when attempting to jive, for example.

Exploring the Outside Environment

The outside environment of garden, street and neighbourhood initially presents more difficulties but, given time, can become as familiar territory to a visually handicapped child as his own home. Once a child becomes mobile, plenty of time will be needed to explore the various terrains through which he walks. Different types of boundary lines may be identified; while the demarcation of pavement from road becomes apparent if the child is allowed actively to discover for himself the different depths of kerb. A two-year-old's method will necessarily differ from that of a five-year-old. The little girl in the illustration finds her method of one foot on the kerb and one in the gutter is also a good balance exercise.

It is stimulating to investigate street furniture through touch activities. By

walking all the way around lamp posts and trees, the child can learn to appreciate their size and their position on the pavement. Letters may be posted in the post-box and telephone calls made from the telephone kiosk. All these objects, once investigated, may further be placed by echo location if the child has no sight. Where the child has some residual vision, this can be used in conjunction with touch to locate objects within the environment.

The weekly visit to the supermarket can be made more interesting to a child if he knows the layout of the shop. It is a good plan for parents to make a special visit to the shop at a time when the weekly shopping is not the prime concern of the outing. The child will then have ample opportunity to examine the contents of the various shelves. As the child feels these items, he should be encouraged to notice any odour that will help identify them, such as the smell of soap in the toiletries section or the smell of cheese at the cheese counter, and so on. A child with some residual vision will be able to use it to pick out any familiar objects, e.g. packets of cereal. The difference between shelves stacked with tins, and shelves with rectangular packets arranged on them may well be identified by children with only minimal vision.

Sound clues can be heard in all supermarkets: the 'click' of the cash register at the check-out points or the hum of the large refrigerators. Once these are located and identified, they will prove valuable clues helping the child to orientate himself within the shop. In fact, most people have a set route that they take through the shop on their weekly shopping visits. This route can be carefully traced by the child during the exploratory visit. On subsequent trips, when he may be sitting in the trolley, he will still be interested in where he is and be conscious of the familiar smells and sounds of different parts of the route.

In addition to the visits to the supermarket, the child should be made familiar with smaller local shops. There is usually a friendly sweet shop in the neighbourhood where the child can learn to find the counter by himself and buy his own sweets. This gives him further opportunity to learn the normal social conventions as he hears his mother chat to the shopkeeper or pass the time of day with acquaintances in the street. The park is an ideal place as there he can encounter other small children and with parents' help, explore the park's play apparatus when it is not too crowded.

Walking

Walking needs continued practice as an exercise in order to improve the child's gait. This differs from 'exploration' walking where the child moves independently. In 'exercise' walking child and parent walk side by side. The parent begins by holding the child's hand that is adjacent to himself with his 'outside hand', putting his free 'inside hand' on the child's back in order to give slight pressure to prevent him from holding his weight back. Without this pressure the child may hang back and allow himself to be pulled along. A good rhythm may be obtained by singing as parent and child walk along. Once the walk is established, the hold can be changed to holding adjacent hands allowing the arms to have a natural swing. As the child grows older, the 'sighted guide' grip may be used (see p. 70), the child holding the parent's wrist or arm depending on which is the more comfortable. By this time the terrain through which they are walking can be discussed, questioning whether the road is flat or hilly, or the path rough or smooth, etc. It is better not to walk independently in these walking practices as the child will soon lose speed and rhythm when left. The object of the exercise is to get him accustomed to a firm steady walk at a reasonable speed which he can maintain without tension. However, 'exercise' walks for young blind children should only be of short duration and always finish with some free movement where the child runs, skips or moves in any way he wishes, at his own independent pace.

A young child can also enjoy the incidental experiences of nature through going for a walk. The feel of rain on his face may be very pleasurable if the walk is taken at a good pace and the temperature is not too low or the walk too long. Wind may be exhilarating when it is at his back blowing him along — quite different from when it is cold and blowing in his face. The different seasons can change the surfaces of the paths walked along and provide interest for a blind child. The crunching noise of dried leaves when walking in the park in autumn, or splashing through puddles on a wet spring day are all natural experiences to be enjoyed. Older children benefit by going for long walks with their parents. One boy aged nine walked part of the Pennine Way during one summer holiday with his father. The child carried his own rucksack on his back and thoroughly enjoyed his holiday. Walking for pleasure is an activity that many blind people enjoy throughout their lives; this experience should be initiated by parents, who may have — or may develop — a taste for it themselves.

Other Activities

A child can be introduced to water activities at a very young age. Children who have been fortunate to have had this early experience with their parents are usually very confident in water and become good swimmers. Water gives support to the body which makes swimming a relaxing activity relieving muscular tension; thus it is particularly important for visually handicapped children to learn to swim as they are so frequently under tension in their day-to-day lives. Swimming makes an excellent family activity where each member can be on more or less equal terms; for this reason most visually handicapped children who have learnt to swim continue the sport as adults within their own families and with their sighted friends.

Horse riding is also an activity that visually handicapped children enjoy but it is expensive if parents have to pay for tuition privately. However, there are many groups of 'Riding for the Handicapped' throughout the country where the tuition is free, and parents should enquire if there is such a group in their area.

Physical activity of any kind gives a visually handicapped child the confidence to move and the enjoyment that this confidence brings; a run in the park, a football game with Dad, a dance with Mum, all aim at the same objectives.

CHAPTER 3

Social Competence and Daily Living Skills

In the last chapter we described activities that parents can initiate to encourage motor skills in visually handicapped children. However, competence in getting around the environment is not enough. Mobility training has to go hand in hand with the education of movement, avoiding 'peculiarities' and acquiring those skills of movement and manipulation which enable a blind person to hold his own in a sighted world.

Mannerisms

There are some movements of the body to which a blind child is particularly prone and obviously enjoys but which, if allowed to continue, can lead to 'blind mannerisms' that are often extended into adulthood. An adult blind person, however much motivated to eradicate a mannerism, may find this an impossible task as the movement is an unconscious one. These movements often appear at times of stress and although acceptable as a comfort for a child, can be a *social* handicap when indulged in by an older person. For example, I know a very able blind adult who circles his head when wishing to make a point in a discussion. Such a mannerism is curiously obtrusive and one can imagine that under certain conditions it could be quite unacceptable — perhaps even a career disadvantage.

Mannerisms in the blind are of two kinds. The first is caused by a desire to move coupled with a fear of moving forward. Twisting round on the spot, violent rocking in a chair, or jumping up and down on the spot are all typical movements exhibited in this type of mannerism. Children who have taken part in the physical activites described in Chapter 2 are unlikely to find the need to indulge in such movements. The second type of mannerism is probably adopted by a child for the relief of stress. Eye poking, head rolling, small rocking movements are examples of this. The majority of young children need some form of comfort, and many sighted small children are 'thumb-suckers', 'chewers' or 'head-bangers'. Some stress mannerisms are carried over into adolescence and are then difficult to eradicate, e.g. nail-biting. Blind children are exposed to a higher degree of stress than their sighted peers, and it is not surprising that they find relief in mannerisms; but the typical forms are different from those of sighted children and therefore set them apart as being 'different'. Being perceived as 'odd' may be a more serious social handicap than the basic handicapping condition itself.

The most common, and the most unacceptable, mannerism is eye-poking, where the head is dropped forward and the closed fist is pushed into the eye socket. Many reasons for eye-poking have been put forward; my own theory is that this closed curled position is a very comforting one. Many sighted people feel secure in the curled up foetal position. The closed fist just fits the eye socket and, since this causes no pain, as would be the case if a sighted person were to adopt this position, the fist stays there. It has been suggested that poking the eye with the finger can induce some light experiences for some children. Many children who have the eye condition of *retrolental fibroplasia* indulge in this particular mannerism and may well get some satisfaction from their activity which then becomes a persistent habit. Whilst parents should try to stop such habits as eye-poking, other, more socially acceptable comforters, must be provided to take their place. A small teddy to cuddle or a favourite piece of rag to chew, even thumb-sucking, is preferable to eye-poking as children outgrow these activities without damaging their appearance. Eye-poking can deepen the eye socket and promote a disfigurement. Other involuntary movements such as rocking or head-rolling should also be controlled through providing alternative activities.

Posture

Just as walking requires exercise and training, so it is sensible practice to encourage a child to adopt a good posture. This is best achieved not by constant 'nagging' but by taking advantage of certain times of the day to see that the child sits correctly. Meal times make a good opportunity for this or story-times when a mother can gently correct the posture of the listening child with her free hand.

The posture of children with minimal vision needs special attention. A child who has defective central vision, for example, will be able to obtain some impression of an object by 'angling' his head so as to throw the image on to the periphery of the retina. He must not be discouraged from doing this because it is important that he makes maximum use of his sight. On the other hand, he cannot be allowed to have his head held permanently to one side. When talking or listening to someone, he must face him directly even if he can distinguish the other person's features more clearly with his head turned: the social consequences of not conforming to custom outweigh the better use of vision. Eating is another example where custom may take preference over the better use of a partially sighted person's vision. A young child's eyes are naturally near to his plate so the difficulty does not arise at this age. However, as the child grows, the plate will be at a greater distance from his eyes, and in order to see his food more clearly, he will instinctively bend over his plate. This position is not socially acceptable and it also encourages a bad posture. The partially sighted person has to learn to eat correctly without closely inspecting what is on his plate with his eyes.

An older partially sighted child may find he can read print if it is held a short distance from his nose or to the side of his 'good' eye. This is to the advantage of the child and must always be permitted. However, the reading material needs to be taken up to the eyes, not the head coming down to the print. In schools for the partially sighted, the desks have adjustable tops so that the work can be raised. Many children prefer to take their heads down, to the detriment of their posture. This preference may well be caused by wrong habits formed when young. Children with minimal vision should be encouraged wherever possible to take objects *up* to their eyes rather than bending over them. Parents can also encourage children to look at objects above them and at a distance from them. Specific exercises of the head and neck, set out in Chapter 4, may need to be practised.

A blind child who adopts a shuffling walk with a poor distribution of body weight is particularly prone to 'flat feet'. It is important to keep a child's feet mobile and this can be achieved through play activities. One activity of value is to hold the child's lower leg just above the ankle and shake it quite vigorously; then the child should be encouraged to practise this exercise; the child can shake the water from his feet in the same manner as he shakes water from his hands. Another activity that will keep the feet mobile is to encourage the child to pick up his socks with his feet. He does this by curling his toes over the sock. Further examples of foot exercises can be found in Chapter 4.

Developing Fine Hand Movements

A visually handicapped person needs to use his hands for tactile discrimination which will enable him to find differences in the texture, shape and size of the different objects that he handles; thus he is able to identify them. He must learn manipulative skills so that he can use objects for his needs. This latter ability is essential for daily living skills where the manipulations required are usually fine movements of the fingers rather than the gross muscular movements of the arms and legs that are used for more active pursuits. Examples of fine movements necessary for daily living skills are seen in such activities as shoe-lacing, the fastening of buttons and the dextrous handling of cutlery.

A child needs first to learn that both hands can work together. Activities that involve bringing both hands together in the mid-line position can be introduced at a very young age. Rhymes such as 'Pat-a-cake, pat-a-cake, baker's man' can be chanted while the mother does the actions holding the baby's two hands. Especially important are the things a child is given to hold and explore with his fingers and become familiar with. In this respect, toys are an important aid in teaching a child the skills necessary for good hand movements. Although a toy is defined in the Oxford dictionary as 'a plaything especially for young children' — a thing meant rather for amusement than for serious use — educationalists have long realised that a child's play with toys is a means of teaching many skills.

Using Toys and Play Activities

Toys by themselves, however, will have little significance for a visually handicapped child beyond what is, or is not, pleasing to the touch. Left to himself, the child's play will consist of momentarily holding the toy, perhaps shaking or sucking it, and then casting it away with no effort to retrieve it. A toy needs an adult to go with it! The parents can initiate the rewarding play that each toy can give. This may be the feel of an interesting shape that the child will experience if he moves his hands over a toy, or a pleasing texture from a soft toy that can be felt not only in the hands but by the cheeks if the toy is rubbed against them. A parent shows the baby how an auditory reward is revealed when he shakes his rattle, and later how the more difficult and precise movements of winding up a mechanical toy will make it move and produce a sound. Parents can teach their children the language that identifies the properties of a toy such as the language of texture (soft, hard, prickly, smooth), the language of shape (round, square, oblong) and the language of size (big, small, tall, short), and so on. This enables the child to identify the properties of his toys and to *rediscover* these properties in the different toys and objects he goes on to handle. The child is incidentally learning an important concept for his intellectual development: the ability to classify objects.

Parents can encourage their baby to reach and grasp for toys. This has the added advantage of giving him an understanding of movement forward in space. A useful method of encouraging a young child to reach for a toy is to have a variety of small toys in a box in front of him. After a period of exploring with his mother, he will learn to reach into the box for a toy and, when he is tired of it, to drop it and reach for another. It is important to have a variety of objects in the box and all of them should be easy to handle; such things as a small soft toy, a homemade rattle, a small 'bendy' toy, a squeezy toy that makes a noise, cotton reels on a string, a teaspoon and a piece of velvet cloth. The variations are endless.

Movements of the hands necessary for daily living skills are often learnt by playing with toys. One movement that blind children find particularly difficult is turning the hands so that the palms face upwards. Many blind children continue to use their hands in the prone position, i.e. with palms facing downwards. This is noticeable in their use of cutlery and when picking up a plate, for example, when they will do so with the fingers on top and the thumb underneath instead of using the reverse way. Using the hands in a turning action can first be introduced in play. One interesting toy that involves this action is a set of 'sound tins'. Each tin in the set produces a different sound when turned over. Another game that gives young children satisfaction is turning over the pages of a large shiny catalogue. Children appreciate the feel of the smooth pages (and sometimes the smell?), and those with a little sight enjoy the bright colours of the pictures. Parents of blind children often make scrap-books for their children, sticking different shapes and textures on to the pages. At first a child will just grab for the page, but as he grows a little older he can be encouraged to put his thumb on top of the page and feel the underneath side with his fingers before attempting to turn it over. Parents should always use this method when turning over any page with their child. The same action of the hand is needed for pouring liquids from one container to another. Water-play using a variety of containers makes an enjoyable game whilst at the same time teaching the pouring action. When handling a dry substance — for example, the child 'helping' his mother to weigh out flour — the use of an egg-cup instead of a tablespoon gives a child something firmer to grasp, and makes the necessary scooping action easier to achieve.

The actions of squeezing and wringing are often experienced in the bath. A sponge makes a fine toy with its soft squelchy feel and water can be squeezed over the body or into a floating container. The wringing action is more difficult because two-handed. It needs to be manually taught by the mother putting her hands over the child's hands and then turning each hand in the opposite direction simultaneously. Flannels are good to practise on.

The desire to build and then knock down would seem to be instinctive in man! Visually handicapped children need to start with large-based objects: shoe boxes, for example, make ideal bricks. Two-inch and one-inch cubes should also be in every toy cupboard. With practice, the child will achieve the exact balance and placement which prevents the bricks from toppling too soon. The well-known 'Stickle Bricks' and 'Lego' blocks have the advantage of locking together for greater stability. Both products also have wheels that can be fixed to the constructions the child builds and this adds further interest. Apart from fitting together there are other methods of assembling things which the child needs to practise. Some things screw together and there are many brightly coloured toys on the market that teach this action. They range from simple plastic bricks that have a hole in the middle which screw on to a rod, to wooden dolls whose limbs can be screwed on and off. Children enjoy screwing on and off the lids of their mothers' empty cream jars; the lingering smell of the former contents gives an added interest.

Shape allows some things to be joined together. Simple large wooden jigsaws enable a child to detect, for example, the concave edge that can receive the corresponding 'jutting out' curve. Here again children need help to do jigsaws. The sequence of first finding the four corners of the jigsaw by feeling for the two straight edges that meet together is in itself an exercise in tactile discrimination. The 'jutting out' piece of a jigsaw needs to be put on top of the corresponding hole and pressed into position; this action will need some help from a grown-up before success is achieved. Jigsaws encourage children with a little vision to use it to the full in order to sort out the pieces.

Modelling is an activity that all children enjoy and it is a very meaningful art form for a totally blind child. Differences in texture can be appreciated by using different mediums to work in; plasticine, for example, has a different feel from wax or clay. All the muscles of the hands are used and consequently strengthened. Two kinds of activity can be experienced in modelling, one in which a representation is made; this the child will learn from models made with the help of a grown-up. These models are invaluable for teaching a totally blind child the concept of wholeness of various objects that are too big to be felt between the two hands, such as a car. The other type of model that a child can make is a less restricted art form where the child creates a shape that is pleasing to him. The latter form of modelling is of equal importance to the first: insisting that each model should represent an object may dampen the child's natural creativity.

Finger painting with thick non-toxic paint is another medium in which a child can experience creativity. It leads on to painting using a fairly thick handled brush. The child can be shown how to hold his brush with a pen-holder grip; this reinforces the correct way of holding his spoon. Shapes can be cut from empty cereal packets and stuck on to cardboard so making a raised surface that can be felt by a totally blind child and then painted. Another method used by teachers of young visually handicapped children is to sellotape leaves on to paper for the child to feel and paint. As he can first collect the leaves for himself this is a very rewarding activity.

Children need a large variety of toys to cover the different aspects of play. Some of these have to be bought and parents can encourage relatives and friends to supply suitable types of toys. Some toys can be made inexpensively, however, or can be everyday objects to be found in the house, like different containers and things to put in them. In many towns there are toy libraries where not only can toys be borrowed but advice on toys and play activities obtained from people with experience of handicapping conditions of different kinds. Parents can help their child by knowing the underlying teaching aspect of the play activity and by playing with their child. However, it is important to remember that for him it must always be a game that he can discard when he has had enough.

Early Training

Self-feeding

The first introduction to self-feeding will be 'finger-eating'. This is an important stage for a blind child; it allows him to feel the texture of different foods as well as to

practise the basic manipulative skills necessary for self-feeding. The child should use his first two fingers and thumb rather than the whole hand to pick up his food. When he takes the food to his mouth it should be seen that his elbow is kept near to his body; this will ensure that he rotates his wrist in order to get the food into his mouth and is a preparation for spoon-feeding. 'Fingers' of bread and butter, chips and pieces of apple are examples of foods suitable for self-feeding.

Spoon-feeding is the next stage. This can begin when the child has the basic manipulative skills to enable him to hold the spoon firmly. He will have already used a spoon in play activities, e.g. for banging with or digging in a sand pit. A very useful technique for teaching spoon-feeding is what has come to be described as the 'backward learning method'; it is used with success in the Infant Department at Tapton Mount School. In this method the child is guided by the mother (or teacher). She takes up a position behind the child and places the spoon in the correct

position between his fingers. She keeps her hands moulded over his and, together, the action of eating is accomplished. This particular action can usefully be broken down into five steps, as follows:

(1) Picking up and holding the spoon.

(2) Taking it to the dish.
(3) Scooping the food from the dish.
(4) Conveying the food to the mouth.
(5) Transferring the food from the spoon to the mouth.

At first the mother does these five movements for short periods before reverting to spoon-feeding the child herself in the usual way. Later on she leaves the child to do the fifth movement alone and then she will gradually work backwards through the steps until the child can do them all himself. Initially, only foods that are easy to handle, like mashed potatoes, are used for self-feeding but gradually more difficult foods are attempted and other items of cutlery are introduced by the same method. When all the above skills have been mastered, the mother may find it helpful to move her hand from the child's hand to his wrist and then to his elbow rather than leave him entirely unaided. This contact with his mother will remind the child what is expected of him in the same way as a sighted child is prompted by seeing that his mother is watching.

Children who have been introduced to the backward teaching method of learning to eat by their parents before coming to school have received a good grounding in an important daily living skill and, above all, do not have to unlearn wrong habits. The basic principle of the method is that the child is taught the correct technique. A young sighted child, for example, will hold the spoon in the grab position and, later, through observation, will change it to a 'pen-holder' grip; a blind child tends to retain the grab position and finds it very difficult to change. This is why the method described above lays emphasis on the child learning the correct grip from the beginning.

Blindness itself does not prevent a person holding and using an implement correctly. The reason that blind people sometimes hold their utensils in an awkward manner is that they have not been taught the basic movements, early manual training can prevent the formation of these habits.

Dressing

The 'backward learning method' can also be used for teaching children to dress themselves. At Tapton Mount, the senior house mother has found that it is easier to begin with garments that pull up such as pants and socks. Teaching a child to put on his own socks is an example of the technique in the following routine. First the child sits on the floor with the mother kneeling behind. Then follow five steps:

(1) The mother puts the sock on the floor with the toe on top facing the child.
(2) She puts the child's hand on either side of the sock with his thumbs inside.
(3) Together they pull the sock over the toes.
(4) Together they pull the sock round the heel.

(5) Together they pull it up the leg.

The progression is for the child to do action (5) by himself and then work backwards through the other actions until he can do them all for himself. Parents are advised to break down in a similar manner each dressing skill into its basic actions and then to teach them in the reverse order as demonstrated above.

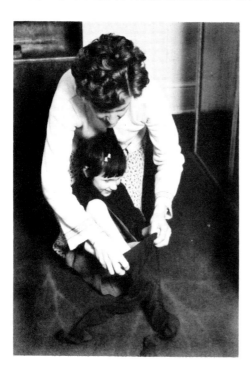 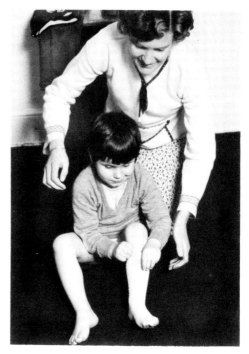

The possession of a 'dressing up' box of clothes not only provides children with scope for imaginative play but stimulates them to practise the skills needed for dressing in a play manner, such as trying to tie a sash or to button up a jacket. Putting on father's boots or mother's shoes and trying to walk in them is a balance exercise as well as fun.

Children should also learn at an early age where to find their own clothes. It helps if a special drawer or chest of drawers can be kept for them so that once they are more or less able to dress independently, they do not have to wait for everyday clothes to be brought for them.

Encouraging Orderliness

Order is very necessary to a visually handicapped person. A partially sighted housewife told me that she did not like other members of her family cooking in her kitchen as they did not always appreciate her need to have everything in a set place. By this insistence on order, she was able to cook efficiently, in an atmosphere of calm, and at the same speed as a fully sighted person.

Once a child knows the environment of his home he should also be taught where things are kept, and encouraged to put things away. Most sighted children are quite willing to drop their things around for their mothers to pick up, but they usually do know where each article should go and at times even have to put them away themselves! Blind children are often not expected to tidy their things away or to be concerned with where household articles are to be found and so many gaps exist in their general knowledge — gaps that a sighted child does not have as he has acquired this information unconsciously by watching his mother tidy up.

Some years ago I was teaching formal mobility to a blind boy of fifteen. The other members of his family were still out when our lesson was due to start but Tom was ready waiting for his lesson — ready, that is, except that he had forgotten to change his shoes; in fact he was wearing 'flap sandals'. I suggested that he should put his walking shoes on but found that he had no idea where they were kept. All he knew was that when he took them off, his younger brother took them away! Eventually we found a large cupboard in the hallway of the flat which served as a shoe-cupboard for the whole family, but was quite unknown to Tom!

Blind children can also be very upset by their inability to find their own toys when they want them. The teaching of orderliness will go some way towards diminishing outbursts and temper tantrums caused by sheer frustration. The little boy in the

accompanying illustration knows exactly where to find his toys in the living room sideboard.

Young children love helping their mother and, if allowed, can learn that all household things have a place. Some things are put away in drawers, others in cupboards, while some articles are on shelves for display. Size and accessibility play a part in this choice of place; young blind children can appreciate this if allowed to explore, for example, the depth of a drawer or the width of a shelf and even, perhaps, to go inside a wardrobe and feel the clothes hanging down. Such activities incidentally help a child to appreciate early mathematical concepts of length, breadth and height in a practical way. If allowed to help organise the placement of their own clothes and toys, blind children will have made a big step forward in independence.

CHAPTER 4

Physical Activities and Games

When a visually handicapped child starts school the training he receives will build on and develop the training begun by his parents: it will become more formal and more sophisticated. But school also offers the opportunity for the development of a range of other physical activities, all of which have a bearing on the child's growing independence and mobility skills. These activities are the subject of the present chapter. No attempt will be made to present a complete physical education syllabus. There is no need for this as visually handicapped children can enjoy a normal programme with a little adaptation, and some modified versions of well-known games are suggested later. To begin with, however, there are certain basic movement skills that must receive special attention if the child is to acquire good mobility and daily living skills.

Exercises to Improve Flexibility

In order to gain an understanding of movement a blind child needs to experience the range of its possibilities — its extreme limits, so to speak. An example of this is the action of curling and stretching. Curling the body into a ball and then stretching out straight is a basic gymnastic movement. The majority of blind children are able to curl up easily but find it more difficult to stretch each limb to its fullest extent. Although they feel stretched, fingers remain curled and ankles and knees are semi-flexed. When the stretching is completed in an upward direction the neck is often not completely extended and consequently the head remains slightly drooped. This is aggravated in the case of a partially sighted child who is trying to use his vision to the maximum by maintaining an odd head position. Three exercises designed to help stretch the upper region of the spine and promote a good head posture are as follows:

(1) The child is asked to lie on his front with his arms at his sides and later, to increase the difficulty of the exercise, with his arms stretched forward. In the latter case the arms are lifted with the body. The upper part of the body is then lifted off the floor and held in this position for a few seconds before returning to the starting position.

(2) The child is encouraged to take a fixed starting position such as sitting with the legs crossed. The back should be straight and the head held centrally; the teacher or parent may need to give manual help to ensure this position. The child then drops his head forward on to his chest, turns it to the left, drops it back, turns it to the right and then brings it to the upright position. (Once the child feels each section of the head movement, slow continuous circling in both directions can take place.)

(3) Turning the head first to the left and giving a quick nod, saying 'Yes!' at the same time, then repeating it to the right, makes an amusing exercise for young children, particularly if followed by a vigorous shaking of the head to the accompaniment of 'No's'!

These last two exercises are of particular value to children who adopt a turned position of the head in order to see more clearly.

Specific practice needs to be given in stretching the other joints of the body. An example of a finger-stretching exercise is for the child to place his two thumbs and first fingers together and press, so that the space between them made by this action contracts; the remaining fingers can be interlaced (see illustration). The action is repeated using the thumbs and middle fingers, the thumbs and ring fingers, and

finally the thumbs and little fingers. This exercise could be followed by alternately clenching and stretching the hands.

In order to make a child feel the full stretch of his knees, he should be directed to sit on the floor with his legs stretched out. He can then press his knees on the floor and make sure that he has left no space that will permit his fingers to get between the back of his knees and the floor. When he has done this he can proceed to other knee-bending and stretching exercises. Care should be taken to ensure that the child feels the stretch of his knees each time.

An example of an ankle-stretching exercise is when the child sits on the floor with his knees stretched forward but with one ankle crossed over the other. The top foot is pressed down towards the floor, moved sideways, upwards, sideways and downwards, thus rotating the ankle joint (see illustration). The action can be taken in a clockwise or an anti-clockwise direction. Walking on tiptoe followed by walking on the heels will enable the child to experience a fully stretched ankle joint and a fully flexed one.

There is a tendency for blind children to walk keeping the foot more or less rigid and inflexible; specific foot exercises need to be given to keep the foot mobile. One such exercise is for the child to sit on the floor with his knees bent and the hip rotated outwards so that the soles of both feet can be placed together; the outer edges of the feet will be touching the floor. The child can feel the 'hole' made by the insteps of both feet. By pressing the toes and heels together and contracting the foot he can feel the 'hole' has enlarged (see illustration).

Correct use of the feet in walking can be encouraged by slow walking where each part of the foot is felt as it touches the floor. First the heel of the forward foot makes contact with the floor, then the outer edge of that foot makes contact, followed by

the big toe. The weight is transferred to the foot and so the child experiences the position where all the weight is on the forward foot. At this stage the heel of the back foot is off the ground but the ball of that foot should still be resting on the floor for balance. The back foot is brought forward and the exercise repeated. It is helpful if the child verbalises his actions, chanting 'heel, edge, big toe, change the weight'. The pace of the exercise is increased as the child feels the movement. There is a machine on the market called 'a rolling road', a form of endless belt. It can be used to teach blind children how to use their feet correctly; it enables them to walk continuously under conditions which eliminate tension.

Blind children miss out on the opportunity to observe and imitate other children. Apparatus can to some extent be used as a substitute, together with a related

commentary by the teacher; the curling and stretching exercise mentioned above, for example, can be carried out on small individual mats (see illustration). The children are told to curl up so that no part of their body is touching the floor. Uncurling the spine can also be practised with the children sitting against the wallbars when they can be encouraged to stretch upwards so that their head touches the next bar above them.

It is important to encourage blind children to jump into space. There are many situations in daily life where it is necessary to thrust forward: when a person is alighting from a train, for example, there is quite frequently a large (vertical!) gap between the step and the platform. Children's confidence can be built up by using apparatus in the safety of the gym, e.g. long-jumping between two mats; the gap can be widened as their jumps improve (see illustration). Children can compete with one another in this type of activity, dropping out as they fail after a prescribed

number of attempts. In competitive activities with a visually handicapped class, it is essential to arrange the children in groups according to the amount of residual vision that they have. When a child reaches his maximum effort and is 'out' he should be able to go straight on to another activity. A blind child cannot improve his standard by watching the technique of his peers.

Movement and Orientation in the Gymnasium

To achieve independent mobility, a child will need to have a real awareness of the different parts of his body together with the ability to relate these parts to external objects. Body awareness in relation to the floor, walls, apparatus and sources of sound is an essential part of movement training as far as a blind child is concerned. By using the floor the child can become aware of different parts of his body. For example, he can first be asked to lie on the floor on his back and then on his front. When he is lying on the floor with his right side touching the surface he can become conscious of every part of his body that is in contact with the floor — the right ear, the right shoulder and arm, the right hip and leg. The left arm and leg will be on top and added interest can be given when the child is asked to lift these limbs in the air to show that they are free.

Teachers of young blind children will find a tambourine very useful when teaching movement. It provides a source of sound to which the children can relate the position of their bodies and helps to teach them rhythm as well. An activity involving the tambourine that I have found to be very popular is first of all to ask the children to stand with their right side nearest to the sound of the instrument. The children listen while I beat a rhythm then move to it keeping their right side nearest the sound. They walk around me in a clockwise direction. I ask the children to obey the sound of the tambourine. When it stops they must stop; when I raise the tambourine higher they must try to move on the same level; when I lower the tambourine they should similarly respond. The activity can finish when the tambourine is dropped to the floor when they must fall down too. Moving in a clockwise or anti-clockwise direction around a teacher who is making a source of sound either by clapping or using a percussion instrument is a good way for visually handicapped children to move at speed in a gymnasium. The children with residual vision in the class can keep well to the outside of the circle and the slower, totally blind, children can come nearer to the sound. Colliding with the subject in front is not as upsetting as bumping head on!

Visually handicapped children should be made aware of the different walls in the gymnasium. One wall may have wall-bars against it, or another a rough brick surface, and so on. In addition, the children should be taught the compass names of the walls; the wall-bar wall may then be associated with perhaps the north, and the rough-surfaced wall with the south. Practice in moving from one wall to another may then be linked with compass direction and the children will have tangible proof, through the wall's distinguishing features, that they have taken the correct path.

In many rooms that children use, it is impossible to get to the corner of the room because of furniture. *We* can see the corner above the furniture in a room but blind children need the experience of feeling the formation of a corner. They must learn through touch that it is the joining of two walls in different directions on the compass and they need, too, to be aware of the angle that is made by the two walls. A simple orientation game to play with children is as follows. First they must be grouped according to sight and ability. The children stand with their own groups which are numbered. The teacher calls a group by number and then names a wall or corner. For example, she might call out, '3 — South wall!' or '2 — North-east corner!' The group called must run to the named place. The game can be played with the children within a group competing to get there first, or the teacher can count to a set number and award one point to each child who gets there within the time. The time allowed can be varied according to the ability of each group.

Walls can be used by a blind child as a means of checking his position when learning to turn. When a sighted subject is asked to turn left, he automatically turns through an angle of 90 degrees and faces a different wall. A blind child does not have this visual aid and must learn a 90-degree turn by its feel. By touching a wall after he has made a turn, he can judge if he has turned correctly. The child should start his turning practice by standing facing the wall; he should check that he is square to the wall by placing the finger tips of both hands against it. After turning left he should ensure that his right hand is in line with the wall; after another quarter-turn he should be able to reach back with both hands and touch the wall; four quarter-turns should bring him back to his starting position. If a child has difficulty in knowing how to start a left turn, I have found it helpful to get him to slap his left side with his left hand, pause, and then face the sound he has made.

Using Large Apparatus

The majority of blind children enjoy and feel safe on large apparatus; some part of their body is always in contact with the apparatus thus providing them with a point in space. Many children, for instance, find climbing a rope or performing continuous somersaults on a bar easier than jumping off a low box. Activities on pieces of large climbing apparatus stimulate children to stretch their limbs and increase their physical stamina; such equipment should be available to all visually handicapped children.

To some degree all visually handicapped people are likely to experience difficulties in balancing; vision is in continuous use to make slight adjustments to balance. It is important for the visually handicapped child to have special training in this skill. Balance exercises can be given where the child's weight is taken on different parts of the body. Standing on one leg, or taking the weight on the head and hands as in a head-stand, are two examples of this form of balance. Competitions between partners of equal strength where one child tries to upset the balance of the other can be an enjoyable way of exercising this skill. A more precise example of this activity is where both partners are hopping and, at the same time, shoulder-pushing each other to try to make their opponent put his foot down first. Progressing along a gymnastic bench is traditionally a standard balance exercise. Blind children may need to practise on the broad side of the bench for a longer period than their sighted counterparts before progressing to the narrow side. A

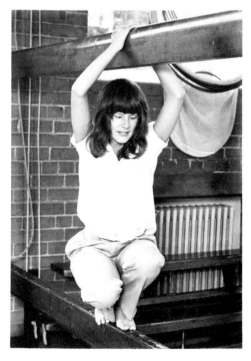

whole set of exercises can be developed from the use of this piece of apparatus including, for example, passing a partner on the bench in as many different ways as possible.

When using a gymnastic beam on which to balance, it is particularly beneficial for the blind child if he is allowed to pull the top beam down to a position where he can stretch his arms up and just touch it (see illustration). If the pegs of the top beam are not inserted the beam cannot be used to bear any of the child's weight; it simply steadies him. In this way he is enabled to perform more complicated exercises which will improve not only his balance but also his gait and body carriage.

Children with good residual vision have little difficulty in gymnastics; their success depends more on natural ability than on visual acuity. I have found that totally blind children who are physically good can vault quite well if allowed to bounce on a spring-board whilst pressing down on the vaulting apparatus with their hands; by this means they get the impetus for a vault similar to that a sighted

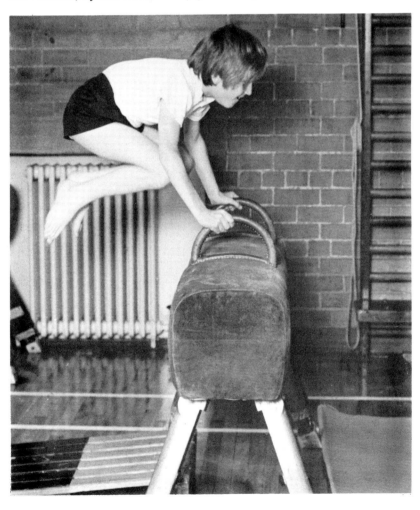

child gets from a run and take-off. This method is particularly useful when the child is performing pommel vaults on a horse or leap-frogging over a buck.

Running Games for Infants

A prerequisite of achieving true independence is the ability to move competently at a good speed. Lack of sight obviously tends to inhibit the pace of movement: it is 'natural' for the blind person to be cautious, to wish to explore the ground one step ahead before committing himself to movement. One of the ways to overcome this reluctance to move is to participate in team games where there is the added excitement of competition. Younger children find excitement in being chased, and games that involve this element are most stimulating. The following games are particularly enjoyable for young blind children.

'Tom Tiddler's Ground'

Ground. Inside; a gymnasium or hall with four large gymnastic mats is sufficient. If the game is played outside, two different adjoining surfaces such as a concrete path and grass are required.

Procedure. The children stand on the mats or the distinctive surface. The teacher tells them she is Tom Tiddler and that they must stay in their garden where they are and not come into her lovely orchard to play. She keeps up a running commentary on her actions such as, 'I'm going off for a cup of tea now! Remember what I've told you!' A few seconds later she calls out, 'I'm coming back now. I hope those naughty children are not in my orchard!' Of course some of the children will trespass on to the surface representing Tom Tiddler's orchard and, with great excitement, will be chased back by the teacher.

This game allows the timid child to make short sorties from 'home base' at first and then gradually become increasingly daring.

'What's the Time, Mr Wolf?'

Ground. This game can be played indoors or outdoors provided that along one edge of the playing area there is a wall or path which will act as a safe 'home base'.

Procedure. The children line up on the path facing the grass or if playing indoors, with their backs to the wall. A child is chosen as Mr Wolf and he stands a yard or two in front of his companions with his back towards them so that they are all facing in the same direction. Mr Wolf walks forward and the children follow him chanting, 'What's the time, Mr Wolf?', whereupon Mr Wolf stops and tells them the time. This is repeated until Mr Wolf suddenly shouts 'Dinner time!' The children must then turn round rapidly and try to reach the home base before Mr Wolf can touch them.

Comments. The children are encouraged to turn immediateіy on the words 'Dinner time!' Practice can in fact be given by the teacher in calling 'Dinner time!' when the children turn on the spot seeing who is the last to turn right round.

It is a rule that the Wolf must call 'Dinner time!' if he reaches the opposite boundary wall without calling out the cue words.

'Big A, Little A'

Ground. This is the same as in the last game.

Procedure. Once again a child is chosen, this time to be a cat and he curls up on the ground about fifteen yards in front of the other children but facing them. If the game is played in a room he will probably be positioned at the opposite wall to the one where his companions are waiting. The children chant the jingle: 'Big A, little A, bouncing B, the cat's in the cupboard and he can't catch me!' As they chant they perform the actions: for 'Big A' they stand in the stretch position with their arms above their head; for 'Little A' they crouch down, and for 'bouncing B' they jump on the spot. When they get to the words 'the cat's in the cupboard and he can't catch me' they tiptoe forward. The jingle is repeated twice and on the second 'me', the cat jumps up and runs after the children who turn round and race back to their home base. An added incentive is to ask the children how near the cat they dare go.

There are many similar games that can be adapted to be played with young blind children. I have found that when playing these traditional games it is advisable to give definite directions where they should move so that they all move the same way; this helps to prevent collisions.

Ball Games for Juniors

Blind children have to react to sound so that those games that involve a ball introduce an added dimension and give the child experience in relating movement to sound. Four games for junior-age children are suggested, arranged in order of progression, that will afford practice of this extra skill.

'Circle Push Ball'

Apparatus. A football should be made 'audible' by the insertion of dried peas or lead pellets.

Procedure. The children should be arranged in circles of six, standing astride with their feet touching the feet of the child on either side of them. They propel the ball along the floor with their hands trying to get it through the legs of any other player. The children try to prevent the ball from going between their own legs by pushing it back with their hands.

A player is 'out' if the ball has passed between his legs, and he then leaves the circle. The remaining children close in to fill the gap thus made. Players who have been eliminated can stand outside the circle to field the balls that come through; in this way they are still part of the game.

'The Number Game'

Apparatus. A football, not necessarily audible, is required.

Ground. The game is best played outside where there is a large area of running surface.

Procedure. All the players are numbered. The teacher stands in the middle of the playing area and calls a number which she continues to call until the player, whose number it is, reaches her. The player now grasps the ball and shouts out 'Stop!'. All the other players who have been running away from the teacher's voice now have to stop immediately. The player with the ball is allowed to take two paces towards any player and then bowl the ball at his legs. If the bowler is successful, the player whose legs have been touched by the ball is eliminated from the game, as indeed is any other player whose legs have been hit by the ball bouncing off. The game continues until there is only one player left and he, of course, is the winner.

Comments. If the throwing player's vision is too restricted to enable him to see the others at all, the teacher will go and stand behind the nearest player and clap. Such a throwing player is than allowed *three* paces towards the sound before bowling.

Sometimes the teacher will have to call a few players back who did not halt immediately 'Stop!' was called.

If a lot of children are playing it is advisable to provide some other activity for the players who have been eliminated.

'Beat the Ball'

This game can also be played with older pupils. It encourages players to run parallel to sound rather than directly towards it. Opportunity is also afforded for practice in turning and throwing.

Ground. The game is best played in the gymnasium.

Procedure. The rules can be adapted to suit players of varying degrees of vision within the same game. As only two players are active at any one time the total number involved should not be more than about eight.

The players stand at one end of the gymnasium and must have some part of their body in contact with the back wall (see diagram). One player, the thrower, stands

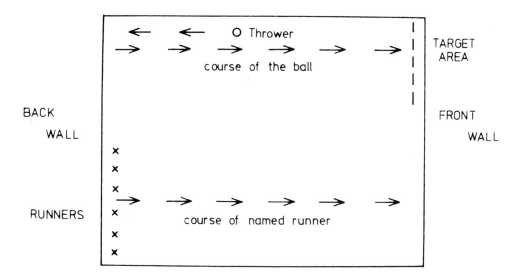

well to the side of them, no more than two feet away from the side wall and a prescribed distance from the back wall which he faces. His distance from the back wall depends on the degree of his vision. He throws the ball at the back wall and at the same time calls out the name of one of the players. It is a foul throw if the name is not called out immediately. The named person runs to the front wall (or target wall) as soon as he hears his name called. The thrower catches his ball from the back wall, turns, and throws it in a direct path to the target area on the front wall (see diagram). A point is awarded to the runner if he reaches the wall before the ball, or to the thrower if the ball arrives in front of the runner. When each runner has had his turn he gets out of the way of the track and the game continues with the same thrower until all the players have been called.

'Danish Rounders'

One game that is particularly good for encouraging visually handicapped children to run freely with speed is a form of 'Danish Rounders'. It can be adapted to suit players of different levels of ability even when they are playing in the same game. As the modifications may be so numerous only the underlying principles are given here rather than exact details. The teacher can modify the game as he or she wishes.

Ground. The game can be played indoors or outdoors. Indoors, the pitch is laid out as in the accompanying diagram. The base mats are large gymnastic mats; the

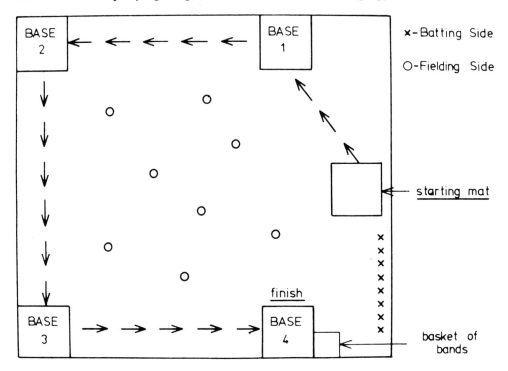

starting mat is a small rubber mat but can be just an area on the floor. Outdoors, the exact position of the base will be governed by the local terrain. A path at right angles to the line of direction taken by the batsmen is an ideal base, as are lines of small mats. Walls can be used but have the real disadvantage of causing the children to slow down their running as they approach.

General Principle of the Game. The game is played between two teams. When played outside, the number in each team is not important; inside, six players on each side is about the limit. There is no bowling in the game except in one variation where the teacher rolls the ball to the batsman; this is rather to give impetus to the latter's hit than to bowl him. The batsman, standing in the starting area, strikes the ball in the manner that he or the teacher has selected for him. He then runs from base to base until he reaches the last one where he will be awarded his rounder. If he wishes he may, without penalty, stay at any intervening base and continue running on another player's hit.

Fielding. All fielders take part in fielding each batsman's hit. The fielder who reaches the ball first stands still and calls out 'One!'; he then passes it to another fielder who calls out 'Two!'. This continues until the last fielder has the ball when he will call out 'Stop!'. By using this technique all the fielders are compelled to run to the place where the ball was first fielded and all of them have handled the ball. Through the calling out of numbers the batsmen are made aware of whether there is time to run to another base.

How Out. A player who is running between the bases when 'Stop!' is called is out. The whole side is out when there is no player ready to bat in the starting area.

Variations. Either a small bell ball or an audible football may be used. A bell ball may be hit with a small 'padder bat' in a manner similar to that used in table tennis; or a stationary ball, either bell ball or football, may be hit with a cricket bat; or the teacher may roll the ball to the batsman. Outdoors, the batsman may hit the ball in any direction he likes. Inside, the batsman must hit forwards over an imaginary line drawn from base 1 to base 4.

If the first fielder to reach the ball finds he is in the path of the batsman, he must move clear after he has called out 'One!' before passing the ball to the next player.

Scoring. It is useful to have a basket of bands at the last base; each batsman can then put on a band when he has successfully completed a rounder. The score for the team is then easily counted at the end of the game. Younger players feel they have achieved something notable when they put on a band.

Modern Educational Dance

Movement is essential to man in two ways. First there is the functional aspect of movement that enables him to travel about, to work, play, and finally, to perform the daily living skills that are necessary for him to use in order to care for himself. Secondly, movement is expressive; through his movement man reveals his culture and his emotions; he presents himself to the world as he wishes to be seen.

Early movement would seem to be almost instinctive. A newborn baby reaches to grasp his mother's breast; a young child will seize a brightly coloured toy. Through watching his parents and taking guidance from them, he learns to perform functional movements with an economy of effort that reduces strain and tension. He also learns to make his movements expressive — pleasing to those who watch him. Lack of sight prevents visually handicapped people understanding the nuances in the movements of others and thereby appreciating the need for graceful movement. Furthermore, a blind subject's movements are often ungainly, though for him they may be functionally effective.

It is possible to teach more graceful movements by using a child's natural sense of rhythm through modern educational dance techniques. The benefit of this particular form of dance is that it gives the child a meaningful movement language that is applicable to any action. It also allows him to experiment with his own movements inside the framework of this language.

Rudolph Laban, who was the innovator of this form of dance, sub-divided movement into the four qualities of *time, weight, space* and *flow.* He was interested in movement in the theatre and in dance, but he also worked in the industrial arena where he suggested less stressful ways for workers to operate their machines. By different combinations of the three qualities of time, weight and space, he evolved the following eight basic actions into which all movements fall:

(1) *Thrusting.* The time quality of quickness, the weight quality of strength and the space quality of direct action.
(2) *Slashing.* Time — quick, weight — strong, space — flexible.
(3) *Floating.* Time — slow, weight — light, space — flexible.
(4) *Gliding.* Time — slow, weight — light, space — direct.
(5) *Wringing.* Time — slow, weight — strong, space — flexible.
(6) *Pressing.* Time — slow, weight — strong, space — direct.
(7) *Flicking.* Time — quick, weight — light, space — flexible.
(8) *Dabbing.* Time — quick, weight — light, space — direct.

Work with children should start by emphasising the different parts of the body and using them in movement sequences based on the qualities of time, weight and space, either stressing one quality in particular or a combination of two or three.

I have found children enjoy making rhythm patterns using their own names. Each child chants his own name in different rhythms; he then chooses the rhythm he likes best and creates a movement sequence to go with it. The steps and the gestures he uses will involve some of the eight actions outlined above. The teacher can suggest further elaborations. She might, for example, encourage the child to repeat his sequence highlighting a different part of his body; or making the sequence into a 'travelling' one, where the child moves through different parts of the room.

Dance Drama

A group feeling can be experienced by blind children when participating in dance drama; both the music and the story will help to make each individual child feel part of the whole. A story that I have found to be a favourite with young blind children is 'Brer Rabbit and the Tar Baby'. Careful organisation is needed when working with blind children: by giving definite directives as to where the children are to move, they later learn to think in terms of space. It also ensures that collisions are less likely so that the children have greater freedom of movement with less tension.

In the above dance drama, for example, the story-teller stands in the middle of the room where her voice gives the dancers a fixed point in space. The class has been divided into rabbits and wolves and each have their corner. The wolves start the action and perform their opening dance in an anti-clockwise direction. Their mime of making a tar baby involves them in moving out to the walls of the gymnasium to reach for imaginary branches and to drag them to the centre of the room. When they have completed this mime they slink off to their own corner, to the accompaniment of suitably sinister music. A lively jig brings the rabbits out of their corner to dance in a clockwise direction around the room. At the end of their dance, they go to the centre of the room where they interact with the imaginary tar baby. They will thus form a fairly close group and when the wolf music brings out the wolves, it is not too difficult for each wolf to find a rabbit. The briar patch is represented by gymnastic mats at one end of the room and the children know the direction to take to reach them. After dragging their victims to the patch and depositing them in it, the wolves once again dance anti-clockwise around the room and return to their corner. After struggling to get free the rabbits emerge and dance clockwise round the room while the wolves stamp with rage in their corner.

Older children who enjoy dancing like to interpret more abstract themes. Poetry and music lend themselves to interpretation through dance.

Many more popular forms of dance can be enjoyed by visually handicapped people. Such activities as country dancing, ballroom dancing and sequence dancing that involve partners are pleasant pastimes for the totally blind and good exercise; they can have a sighted partner and enjoy dancing in sighted company. Dancing is a leisure pursuit that can be continued throughout life.

Other Leisure Activities for Older Students

Apart from dancing, there are many other leisure activities which, although started at school, can develop into life-long interests. Boys and girls who enjoy games are disposed to welcome any physical activity in which they can participate. The more they can experience sporting activities when young, the more likely they are to find a physical activity that they can continue when they are adults.

Travelling through today's busy streets puts pressure on a person with defective vision; he has to have a higher level of concentration than a sighted traveller. This pressure can be eased by regular relaxation periods. Many people are able to relax tense muscles by performing yoga health exercises which, incidentally, lay great emphasis on correct breathing. Yoga is an excellent activity to introduce to visually handicapped adolescents. By this age a student's mobility training is demanding more independent travel by him and, furthermore, it is possible that he has reached a period of rejection of other more strenuous physical activitites, as indeed have many sighted adolescents.

Swimming is also a very enjoyable way of keeping fit. All schools for the visually handicapped in the UK teach children to swim as part of their physical educational programme. Some schools go further and provide opportunities for learning horse riding, ice skating, sailing, athletics and judo under expert tuition. Visually handicapped children sometimes have the opportunity to take part in different sports through the services of enthusiasts who are willing to give their time to introduce these children to their own particular interest. For example, children from Tapton Mount School have been involved in cross-country running, motor cycle pillion riding and water skiing. Some sports which children have met at school are continued by their families at home. Examples of activities that families can enjoy together are sailing, tandem riding, horse riding and hill climbing.

Visually handicapped people themselves have started clubs for the enjoyment of sporting activities. For example, in Bradford the 'Out and About Club' was started

by a group of visually handicapped people, and other groups have been formed in Nottingham and London and other parts of the UK. Such continuation of sporting activities into adulthood is one of the means by which visually handicapped people can enjoy social contacts while keeping themselves fit. Above all, such activities engender in the participants a true independence of spirit.

CHAPTER 5

Mobility Techniques and Training

In the previous chapter we saw how through physical education, including gymnastics, dance, games and sports activities, the visually handicapped pupil becomes physically fit and, furthermore, acquires a body alertness which makes him increasingly responsive to 'clues' within his environment. Thus he becomes more independent. However, to be truly independent within an unfamiliar environment, including the challenging conditions of a busy street, special travel or 'mobility' techniques have to be learnt.

Mobility techniques originated in the United States where, after the Second World War, a rehabilitation centre attempted to solve the problem of independence training for war-blinded Air Force personnel. A team of doctors, physiotherapists and nurses blindfolded themselves and worked with their patients to discover ways of overcoming the problems of living without sight. From this rehabilitation programme techniques were evolved to cover all aspects of daily living; these included arm protection techniques, search techniques, the best way to use a sighted guide, and the technique for using a long cane in order to give the blind individual a clear path when travelling independently. The value of sighted people working under a blindfold in order to appreciate the problems of lack of sight was clearly demonstrated. Later this led to the establishment of a training course for mobility instructors in which they completed the practical part of their training under blindfold.

In the early 1950s the Royal National Institute for the Blind sent the late Dr Alfred Leonard to the US to evaluate the American system of mobility training. He was very impressed with what he saw and as a consequence Mr Stanley Suterko was invited to train some people in the UK. I was fortunate enough to be included in his course. Dr Leonard set up a Mobility Research Unit at Nottingham University and, in addition, a training centre for mobility instructors and teachers was established in Birmingham. Schools for the Blind became interested in mobility and sought to make it a set subject in the curriculum. To further this aim, conferences and working parties were arranged.

During this period it became evident that while the American system of training was ideal for sighted adults who had become blind, blind children — especially those born that way — needed a different approach. The adult blind could learn their mobility with a concentrated period of instruction. At first it was considered appropriate to wait until blind children became sixteen years of age so that they could then take the same course of instruction as the adult blind. This did not lead to very satisfactory results except where children had been born with sight, were physically able, had good average intelligence and were highly motivated. In many instances it was found that blind adolescents used their mobility skills when at school but reverted to dependence on parents when at home. The attainment of independent mobility and the acquisition of self-help skills depend on the contribution of the parents and the gradual build-up of the necessary techniques. It must also be observed that blind children have some advantages over recently blinded adults and over sighted people under a blindfold which need to be utilised to the full. Because of their total lack of experience of sight they are not worried about not seeing and, moreover, they absorb non-sighted clues more easily than those who are still relying on their memory of what they have seen.

If formal mobility training is introduced when the child is about ten years old, he can still treat the lessons as a game and laugh when things go slightly wrong. For example, a ten-year-old girl who accidently sat on someone's lap when seeking a place on a bus treated it as a great joke. If an adolescent youngster had had the same experience it would have been an embarrassing disaster. Not least among the advantages of early teaching is the fact that young children have great faith in their parents and teachers and will accept the standards that are set for them. Incidentally, those who teach these children need to ensure that they do not set too *low* a standard. Furthermore, as each skill is acquired it must become part of the accepted way of living.

Specific Mobility Techniques

The techniques of mobility and daily living skills that were first taught in the United States are in themselves excellent but need to be introduced gradually. There is no correct order of presentation; they should be learnt and used as the need for them arises which will vary from individual to individual. They are set out here together with comments based on my experience of teaching them to young children.

Trailing

Trailing is effected with the back of one hand brushing an object that is at the side of the subject. The finger tips should be curled to protect the nails and the hand positioned in advance of the body. Trailing can be used along a wall, or when negotiating an obstacle that is in the subject's path. Later in formal mobility it is used as a safety precaution to trail across the front or back of a stationary car before crossing a road or trailing the outside of a bus in order to locate the entrance. Young blind children will often instinctively trail by putting both hands on, for example a

wall, and walking sideways. They often use this method when holding the bannister of a stairway. This method of trailing is not to be encouraged as it tends to induce a poor gait. Practice in the correct method can first be given by holding one of the child's hands while he trails along a wall with the other. Parents can provide young children with experiences of trailing in many other ways: as, for example, finding the doorway of a shop when the door is flush with the shop window or trailing along the side of a child's bed towards the pillow to find the top of the bedclothes.

Arm Protection

There are two arm protection positions, one for high objects and one for low objects. For protection against high objects the arm is raised forward to shoulder level and the forearm is bent so that the palm of the hand comes into line with the opposite shoulder. The palm of the hand can be turned so that it is facing away from the body. If the object likely to be encountered is an overhanging bush, the forearm should be raised to cover the face. It is important to keep the upper arm extended and the forearm well forward.

For protection against low obstacles the arm is held downward in a straight position diagonally across the body and in advance of it. By using both arms, one in each of the above positions, double protection can be obtained. It is particularly important for visually handicapped people to take the high arm position when approaching a doorway; a half-open door is a hazard even to those with good residual vision and the sharp edges of the door can provide a disconcerting bump. I have found the high arm position difficult to teach to congenitally blind children. Instinctively they feel safe when they have both arms held forward at shoulder level; this gives them a feeling of security. Unfortunately, it creates a false sense of security for they can walk into obstacles that pass between their arms. One method that I have used with some success is to ask the child to touch one shoulder with his opposite hand, then to raise his elbow and move his hand forward. The position needs a lot of practice as the congenitally blind child tends to lose the position of the hand once it has lost contact with the shoulder. The exercise of walking towards an open door with the arm in the correct position will show a child how he can save himself from being hurt.

Search Techniques

One of the frustrations for a visually handicapped person is his inability to retrieve quickly objects that he has dropped. The only way to minimise the irritation created by such situations is for the visually handicapped person to learn a set procedure to cover the ground systematically. By introducing blind children to search procedures in a game form they are more likely to use them when the need arises in daily living situations. One search game is to have the child drop a coin on to a hard floor surface and then discover how he can retrieve it. He does this by dropping down quickly and placing his hand where he heard the coin touch the ground. If the coin rolls he should follow the sound until it stops. When his hand does not come in contact with the coin he should move it in ever-widening circles until the coin is located.

A game of 'Hide and Seek' with a toy can interest a child and teach him to search systematically. He could, for example, be told 'Teddy is on the bed; see if you can find him'. He is advised to start at the pillow end of the bed and to run his hand over to the other side, to go back and forward across the bed gradually moving to the foot end. Through such games the parent can teach a child to find things he wants in a methodical way. It must not be forgotten, however, that the child needs a lot of practice in real situations. It is so much quicker for a parent to pick up the dropped toy or to get the pyjamas from the bed! Though it takes longer the child should be allowed to do things for himself.

The technique for finding things on the table at meal times should be taught and practised. The principle is to keep the fingertips in contact with the table as the hand moves. For example, to pick up a glass of water the finger tips should be placed on the table edge then moved forward until they come in contact with the glass. One way of describing the position of objects on the table in relation to a blind person is to use the markings on the clock. This is used for describing the positioning of food on a blind person's plate. For young blind children, however, who are not yet able tell the time, it is preferable to leave them to find the position of the food through touch; meat has a very different texture from potatoes which can be discerned by a spoon or fork. When giving instructions on locating objects on the table the use of such phrases as 'directly in front of you' or 'to your left' is simpler than using the clock-face analogy.

Squaring Off

This technique ensures that a blind person is squared to an object and it is an essential part of mobility training. When a blind person moves independently he must have some means of ensuring that he is going in a straight line. Squaring off can be achieved when any two limbs are touching the base obstacle. For example, standing with both heels touching the wall will enable a blind person to start his walk across the room in a straight line. Alternatively he could use both elbows reaching back, or two hands touching the wall, with the same results. One of the important applications of this technique is used when sitting at the table. The blind person should put the finger tips of both hands on the table with the first fingers touching. Then he should move his hands out to shoulder width; by this method the subject can tell whether he is sitting square to the table. If children are taught this at an early age good habits will be formed.

Children should practise using different limbs with which to square off. The heels are useful against a wall or carpet edge, while the backs of the calves are important for squaring off to a chair before sitting down. Incidentally, instruction in the correct way of sitting down will need reinforcement as a child gets older. Most children climb into chairs without thought and their manner of sitting is not of particular importance to them. Unfortunately, many blind adults seat themselves in a most ungainly way. Practice needs to be given in the art of sitting down in a graceful manner. Once a subject has located the seat of the chair he should stand straight using his legs to keep in contact with it. He can then turn so that both calves are touching the front edge of the chair thus ensuring that he is square to it; he can then sit with confidence. Having sat down he should run the fingers of each hand to the outer edges of the chair to make sure that he is centred: if necessary he can then re-adjust himself. This manner of sitting down needs practising but it is well worthwhile as it gives a more pleasing action than so often displayed by blind adults who turn in a bent position keeping their hand on the seat.

Centring

Just as the subject must learn to centre himself in a chair, so it is important for blind people to use their fingertips to check their positions in relation to objects in front of them. Centring is a response likely to follow on from squaring off when sitting down at the table. The subject not only needs to be squared to the table but centred in relation to his cutlery. Again, a child needs to check the edges of his Brailler with his fingertips to ensure that he is centred in relation to it. He will be able to find objects on his desk more easily and can preserve an order in their placement. For example, he can then put his textbook on the left side of the desk and his completed work on the right, if he centres himself in relation to the Brailler.

Lining Up

This technique is used for taking a direction line from an object. The blind person lines up alongside one object in the trailing position in order to give himself a line of direction towards another point in the room. For example, a subject might line himself up with the side of the settee before moving to the door as he knows this would place him on the correct line. A person can also use a similar technique with sound; for example, when walking along a road a blind person can use the sound of passing cars to line up with in order to maintain a good line of travel. One exercise I give to children in a mobility lesson is to tell them to stand and face the traffic on a fairly busy road. I ask them to wait until a car passes on the side nearer to them and then to turn to face in the same direction as the car. When the next car passes them they move forward with it; as they continue down the road they make use of the sound of each car that passes to ensure that they are walking parallel to the traffic.

Room Exploration

To understand the dimensions and layout of a room, a blind person needs to undertake a systematic search of the whole room. He should first trail the walls starting and finishing at the door. From this initial activity he will learn the shape and size of the room, the location of the windows and fireplace and the position of any furniture that is against the wall. Having completed his exploration and returned to the door he should then move to the nearest corner and stand with his back against the wall. He takes a pace sideways and crosses over to the other side of the room. On reaching the opposite side he should turn, square off with the wall, take another step sideways and repeat the process until the whole room is covered. In this way the subject becomes aware of the furniture in the room and can use this information to orientate himself. People who have had sight do not find it difficult to reconstruct a visual picture in their minds after doing this exercise; they have a visual memory of many rooms that gives them a form of reference. Totally blind children who have never seen, and children whose sight has never been sufficient for them to perceive a room as a whole, need more help. It is essential that such children make a plan of the room under investigation as they explore it. Initially such plans should be in 3-D form but later, when children have had some experience in representation, plans may be made in 2-D form using 'Melinex' paper and a small mapping wheel that embosses a raised line when used on a Dunwell Frame. (A ball-point pen has the same effect.)

When making a 3-D plan the teacher must first see that he has a suitable base for the plan and blocks of some kind to represent the furniture. I use a magnetic board as a base. This is a tin sheet backed with cardboard to make it rigid. The edges of the board, bound with tape, represent doors, windows and furniture. A piece of magnetic rubber is attached to each block which is then held in position on the board. The children are familiar with the different size of blocks as they use them in number work, so I am able to use the smallest block, the 'white brick' as it is known, for chairs, and the next size, the 'pink brick', for doors. To distinguish other furniture, I label the longer blocks using 'Vito' embossing foil.

A set of 'Lego' bricks and bases also make ideal material with which to make a 3-D plan of a room. If the room is irregular in shape, having, for instance, a bay window, a line of blocks may be built round to represent the walls and the bay; a gap can be left for the door. Lego bricks are useful when teaching the scale of a room or building. The children can measure the length of the walls by using an audible measuring wheel; each Lego brick can then represent a fixed length. Children who have a little sight can also use the top surface of their table as a base for a map of their classroom. For totally blind children this is not very satisfactory as the objects put on the table to represent furniture are so easily displaced.

Whatever the material chosen to make a plan of the room it is a great advantage if the children have had the opportunity to become familiar with it through play, prior to making the plan. When they come to the task they need to concentrate on interpreting the room rather than getting to know the materials they are using. The first plan that a child makes should be of a room that he knows very well. For example, if he is at boarding school he could start by making a plan of his dormitory. After the plan is made, there can be discussion over such things as whose bed is nearest the window or whose bed is on the opposite side of the dormitory.

After this, a room that is unfamiliar should be explored and a plan made. Eventually the child will be able to locate different parts of the room by referring to his plan. Next, the child can put a small doll within the plan and move it around. I tie a ribbon on the doll's right hand to help the child to become aware which side of the doll is nearest to different items of furniture and which way the doll has to be turned to move to different parts of the room. The most important feature of a room is the position of the door so that the child can find his own way out. Through playing with a doll in a 3-D plan a child can learn to relate different items of furniture to the door, and by insisting that the child moves his doll to items of furniture and then brings it back to the door, the teacher can encourage him to make this part of his own routine when learning a new room.

The final stage in this progression is reached when a child is able to interpret a plan made for him by someone else. A further activity children enjoy is to make a plan of a room and then hand it to another child for him to locate different toys within the room placed in named places. Meanwhile the child is following someone else's map and instructions.

A blind person makes use of non-sighted clues to orientate himself within a room (as discussed in Chapter 1). Blind children who are too young to appreciate the concept of plan making can be helped to learn their way about a classroom if the teacher places sound clues in a meaningful way. The importance of knowing how to reach the door from any part of the room has already been stressed. The teacher can assist them in this by hanging bells on the back of the door and at specific times asking the children to turn and face the door when it is opened. So while they are in different parts of the room the children, subconsciously, become aware of the position of the door when they hear it opening.

Young blind children get to know a room through playing in the different parts of it. Most classrooms are divided into different play areas such as the water play area, the sandtray area and the book corner. Motivation plays a large part in how quickly a child finds a particular part of the room; the way to his favourite activity will be learnt first!

A mobility tape is another useful stimulus. The tape carries instructions to the child to fetch articles from different parts of the room and to bring them to his desk. This activity should be carried out during a work session when the room is quiet and when children cannot receive clues from the sound of other children playing in the places that they must visit. Such an exercise will enable the teacher to discover the parts of the room with which each child is unfamiliar and subsequently she can give more help.

Introducing the Sonic Torch

In the preliminary stage to formal mobility training, children can still be taken in small groups. When formal mobility training is started this will be changed to a one-to-one relationship. Whilst still working in a group situation part of the lesson can be set aside for activities that introduce children to the sonic torch. This is a hand-held aid that detects objects in advance of the user (see p. 7). Examples of classroom activities are as follows. First the children scatter in the room and stand still; the child with the torch searches for his companions using the aid. He tries to circle round each subject he locates without touching them. The second exercise is to have two children stand with a gap between them while another child using the sonic torch tries to walk through the gap. In the third example, he runs about in a space outside while another child, using the torch, tries to keep up with him.

The Silva Compass

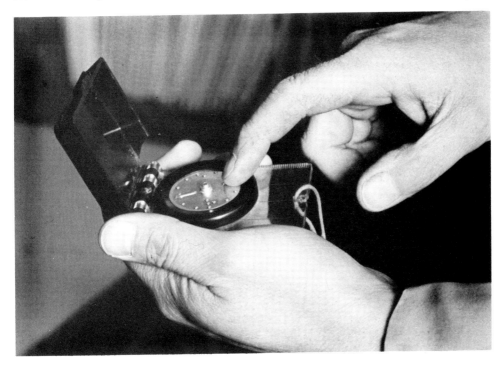

Another piece of orientation apparatus that can be introduced at this stage is the Silva Compass. This is an instrument where the points of the compass are embossed in Braille. The compass must be held still and flat in the hand while the user counts up to ten before opening the lid and reading the Braille markings. Once the child has mastered this he can use it as an aid to making a plan of the school campus on a magnetic board.

Sighted Guide Techniques

One of the most important mobility aids for the blind is a sighted person. The use of a sighted guide need not detract from the blind person's independence and he has to learn how to make best use of such an 'aid'. The following techniques were devised in the US to enable a sighted person to assist a blind subject in the most acceptable way.

The Basic Grip

The blind person should hold the guide's arm just above the elbow with his thumb on the outside of the arm and his fingers curled round the guide's upper arm (see illustration). This position will enable the blind person to walk side by side with his guide but half a step behind.

Although one usually holds a blind child by the hand as it is a more friendly position, there is a place for using the sighted guide hold when taking children out in the town. When the technique is used with a small child it will probably be more comfortable for him to hold just above the grown-up's wrist. A mother may have two children whom she is taking out plus a shopping bag. The sighted guide grip can just as well be used on the side of the shopping bag leaving the free hand for the sighted child. The technique is often useful when going for a brisk walk as it is easy for a rhythm to be created between the parent and the child in this close position. It is important not to let the child drag on the held arm; this can be tiring for the parent and is bad for the child; a light grip and a steady pace should be encouraged.

Narrow Gaps

There will be times when the guide can see that there is not room for the two of them to proceed abreast. He can indicate that this is so, to his blind companion, by pushing the elbow of his gripped arm backwards. His partner should respond to this movement by stepping back behind the guide and straightening his arm. They will then be walking in single file position; the blind person will also be a full step behind and will thus avoid treading on his guide's heels. When the pathway permits it, the guide brings his elbow to his side and the blind person steps forward once again.

When taking a child through rather crowded streets it is important that the guide and the child should have practised the single file position. Sighted shoppers expect children to give way for them and may not realise that the child cannot see. The child may also initiate the movement of stepping behind if he feels unsafe.

Changing Sides

Sometimes the guide may feel that it is advisable for his companion to be on the other side. This can be done without stopping. The blind person crosses over behind his guide keeping contact with the latter's back by trailing first with the hand with which he has held the guide's arm, and then changing to the other hand which should come in contact with the guide's other arm at the correct place. For children, practice should begin in a stationary position before trying it 'on the move'. Subsequently, children enjoy changing while the guide is walking quickly and even when they are both running.

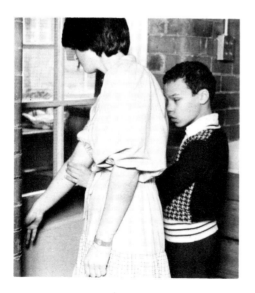

Going Through Doorways

When going through a doorway it is more convenient if the guide has the blind person on the hinge side of the door. If necessary, therefore, he asks him to change position. The guide opens the door using the hand of his gripped arm; this allows the blind person to become aware of where the handle of the door is and which way the door is opening. The guide then walks through the doorway leaving the blind person to shut the door using his free hand. Children experience little difficulty in following this procedure and when it is practised in unfamiliar surroundings they enjoy feeling different types of door handles.

Stairs

The guide should warn his companion when they are approaching stairs and say whether the stairs are ascending or descending. The guide should see that both he and the blind person are square to the bottom (or top) step and then pause before stepping on to it. The blind person will be able to interpret the new movement because his arm will be taken slightly forward and upwards if the stairs are ascending; if the stairs are descending, he will feel his arm being taken forwards and then downwards. He will then follow the guide but will always be one step behind him (compare with the cane technique described on page 78). Again, through the

movement of the guide's arm, the blind subject will know when his partner has reached the top or the bottom of the flight of stairs and he will realise that he has one more step to negotiate. If there is a hand rail or bannister the guide needs to ensure that the blind person has grasped it with his free hand before starting. It is, however, essential to practise without the assistance of a rail so that the subject is prepared for situations where no rail is available.

Children need a lot of practice in order to negotiate stairs with ease; the use of a sighted guide method gives them confidence. Emphasis should be put on the fact that the guide is one step in advance. This can be further reinforced by the child saying 'You!' when he feels that the guide has reached the top, followed by 'Me!' when he has reached it.

Taking a Blind Person to a Chair

When a guide is taking a blind person to a chair, he always puts the hand of the arm that is being held on to the back of the chair. The blind person can then run his hand down until he is in contact with the chair; the guide then leaves him to find his own way to sit down. The blind person will know where he is, in relation to the chair, through touch. For example, if the chair has been approached from the front, he will feel the front of the chair with his legs and will lean forward. If he finds he is at the back of the chair, he can trail it to the front by himself. The action of seating has been described earlier (p. 65).

Taking a Blind Person to a Seat in a Theatre or Cinema

The guide should enter the row first, face the front while the blind person follows and also turns to face the front. Both of them then sidestep until the seats are reached; the guide stops and the blind person feels the seat with the backs of his legs. They disengage when the seats are reached, the blind person seating himself. To go out, the guide first passes in front of his companion so that again he is leading; together they make their exit with the same sidestepping action. On leaving the row they will be facing the stage; the easiest way to turn is for them to break contact, first turning inwards to face each other and then turning to face the exit.

Parents, relatives and friends of visually handicapped people soon understand the advantages of using these sighted guide techniques. But the general public also need to be aware of the correct way to offer help to a blind person. Nevertheless, when a blind subject is travelling independently and needs such assistance it is his responsibility to ensure that he is helped in the correct way. The underlying principle of the sighted guide technique is that the blind subject *takes the arm of the guide* rather than the guide holding him. By doing this, the blind person takes the initiative; it is he who decides when he needs assistance and when he does not.

Although this may appear to be a trivial matter, fundamentally it is essential to the independence of the blind person. So many well-meaning helpers will seize the blind person and push him in the direction they think he should go; they have even been known to leave him in the middle of a busy road! The instructors at the rehabilitation centre at Hines, Illinois, felt this to be an issue of such importance that they devised a special technique that a blind person could employ if a member of the public continued to keep his grasp on the on the blind subject's arm in spite of being asked to change. This technique is called the Hines Break; the blind person simply swings his held arm forward and upward in one swift movement, thus breaking the grip. Children show little embarrassment when getting assistance from the public. With practice, they can be polite but firm in ensuring that the correct grip is taken before allowing themselves to be escorted across the road.

Cane Technique

As indicated earlier, the technique for using the Long Cane was evolved in the Armed Services for the war-blinded. A point of more than superficial interest is that the swinging movement of a Long Cane in front of the user was derived from the operation of the war-time mine detector.

The cane is held in a central position by the preferred hand of the subject. It is held so that it reaches the ground one-stride's distance in advance of the user's feet. It is swung in an arc while walking so that when the right foot is forward, the cane will be to the left and when the left foot moves forward the cane will be swung to the right. This ensures a two-stride clearance for each foot. The ends of the arc traced out by the cane should finish on the ground about one inch beyond the line of the subject's shoulders. The cane thus acts to its user as a cat's whiskers serve the cat: the subject is assured of a clear path for his shoulders as well as for his feet.

There are several varieties of the Long Cane on the market; some of these are rigid and some of them can be folded. Common to all canes, nevertheless, is a long rubber grip, like the grip on a golf club, and a removable tip at the bottom of the cane. The tip wears out from rubbing against the ground and needs to be easily replaceable. Different shaped tips can be bought and, according to which shape is used, the swing of the cane may vary slightly. It is essential that the cane is the correct size for its user; when placed vertically it should reach from the ground to nearly the top of the breast bone.

Children whose sight is such that they cannot see the edge of the pavement without peering downward need the aid of a Long Cane. The factors determining when a child should start training are dependent on his ability to walk with a steady gait and having sufficient control in the wrist and arm to hold the central position and to control the movement of the cane. The cane should first be introduced in a hall or gymnasium where the floors are smooth and there is likely to be at least 15 metres of clear walking space from one wall to another.

Holding the Cane

When teaching a child with a small amount of vision or one who has had sight at one time, the instructor should stand opposite him holding out the cane with the grip towards him and ask him to shake hands with it. The instructor should make sure that it is in the centre of his body. The index finger will then need to be adjusted so that it lies straight down the grip of the cane. Congenitally blind children will have difficulty in maintaining a correct grasp of the cane and will need more help. In such cases, success is more likely to be achieved if the following procedure is followed. The child should be asked to put both his hands together in front of him, fingers straight and thumb on top; this will bring his hands to the midline body position. The instructor will then put the cane into the child's hands so that it is lying in a straight line from the fingertips to the heel of the hand. the instructor then places the tip of the cane on the floor ensuring that the cane is straight and that the tip is forward and in line with a spot between the feet. The child is asked to curl his other fingers and thumb of the preferred hand around the cane; he should then be able to feel the fingers in the palm of his other hand. Maintaining the position of the hand grasping the cane, he can lower the other one.

Initial Steps

The child should begin his practice by squaring up against one wall and walking across the room to the other wall keeping the cane in the central position (see illustrations). The teacher may need to walk with him, his hand over the child's

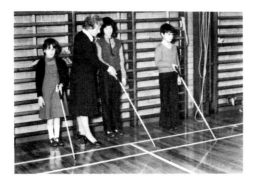 

hand that is holding the cane. This exercise enables the child to get the feel of walking forward with an implement without straining it out ahead; his own momentum is all that is required. As soon as the cane touches the wall, or any other obstacle on the opposite side of the room, he is told to loosen his grip and let the cane fall to the vertical position; he will now be holding it by his thumb and two fingers. Repeating the exercise to and fro across the room, the child's attention can be drawn to the maintenance of a straight path. A regular speed prevents veering and, to reinforce this, the teacher can give the point to which the child directs his footsteps by clapping from across the room. When the child has achieved a regular

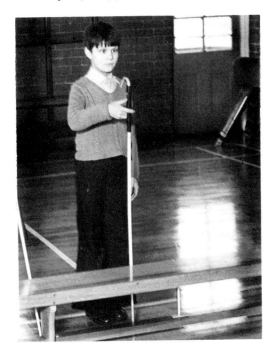

rhythm, the teacher can remain quiet; the child can judge by the distance he is from the teacher at the end of his walk the amount he has veered off course, if at all. A further exercise to practise the release of the cane when it comes in contact with an obstacle is for the child to walk while maintaining the central position of the cane along any direction in the room. When he contacts an obstacle he lets the cane go to the vertical position and is told to notice how high up the cane the obstacle comes. This is a way of assessing the height of the obstacle encountered. He can also feel the texture of the obstacle and guess what it is. He turns in a new direction and repeats the exercise.

Swinging the Cane

When the child is used to the central position of the hand, he is ready to be taught how to swing the cane. It is advisable to introduce this in a stationary position.

Many a congenitally blind child is unable to match the distance of one inch outside each shoulder to the same distance on the floor. Help can be afforded in such cases as follows. The child is asked to lie down on his front and put a bean-bag just outside each shoulder. He can then feel the required distance and, later, use the bean-bags as markers. Another useful method is for the teacher to stand in front of the subject with her feet spread apart at the correct distance. The child then swings the cane using the teacher's feet as markers; from this position the teacher can hold the child's hand centrally as he swings the cane.

The teacher should try to impart the same rhythm for the cane as she gave for the walk; for the swing and the walk are now to be synchronised. If the child is given the opportunity to have a few practice walks across the room without having to worry about synchronising the feet and cane but concentrating just on the rhythm, he becomes more relaxed and achieves a more rhythmic swing. The child is then asked to square up to a wall, centre the cane and say with which foot he is going to start his walk. As he steps forward with the preferred foot, he moves the cane in the opposite direction. It may be necessary, at first, for the teacher to walk with the child, holding his cane hand until he is walking rhythmically, when the teacher can release her hold. If the child gets out of step, he should be stopped and asked to start again. Here, once again, a clapped or counted rhythm helps the child to walk evenly. Once he has got the feel of starting off correctly taking his initial step with the preferred foot, he should practise using the other foot for this purpose — the cane will, of course, then have to be moved initially in the opposite direction. Progression comes in a further exercise when the child starts to walk with the cane in a central postion but just off the floor; he then picks up the swing of the cane while he is in motion. This is to prepare him for those occasions when the cane is stopped, for example by a crack in the pavement; the walker will not want to stop on each such occasion in order to restart the cane on the correct foot.

Negotiating Stairs

Blind children need to learn a routine method of ascending and descending stairs. The cane is used as an aid in going up and down stairs following the same principle that obtains when the sighted guide method is used (see p. 73): the cane, like the guide, must be one step in advance of the visually handicapped person.

When the child encounters the bottom stair when *ascending*, he allows the cane to go to the vertical position, dropping his hand to the bottom of the grip; he notes too the height of the stair. By moving the cane from side to side along the edge of the stair, he ensures that he is squared off. With the cane held centrally and hanging vertically, the subject lifts it so that the tip is against the top edge of the second step; this action will necessitate the straightening of the cane arm. As the subject's foot comes on to the first step the cane will touch the front edge of the third step. This will continue until the top of the stairway is reached when the cane 'misses' because there are no more steps; the child will then know he has one more step to take. The most common fault by any child learning this technique is for him to bend the cane arm; this will bring the cane and the foot on to the same step and rob him of advance warning of the top step. Blind children generally find this means of ascending stairs comparatively easy to learn and very satisfying; the cane makes a nice 'clicking' noise on uncarpeted stairs and children enjoy moving up quickly.

Some blind children find the technique of *descending* stairs more difficult to learn; they are reluctant to let their weight be carried forward. Warning is given of a descending stair when the child feels his cane go over the edge of the step. He will immediately hold his cane still and move forward to the edge of the stair. He squares off to the top edge of the step by moving the cane from side to side keeping it in contact with the same step. He then lets the tip of the cane touch the flat surface of the next step down, thereby learning the depth of the stair. He moves the cane along the flat surface of this step thus obtaining information on the width of the stairway; then lifts the cane slightly away from the edge and begins his descent. His arm will be extended in the usual cane position, and when the cane touches the ground at the bottom of the stairs, he will know that he has one more step to take.

The action of descending stairs needs more practice than ascending. The cane must not be allowed to drift upwards but should point steadily forward and downwards. The teacher will need to steady the cane in the correct position until the

child can do this for himself. The child should practise first on familiar stairs where he can check the position of his cane and foot without much tension; later he can move on to practise on unfamiliar stairs of different depths and widths.

Using a Guide Line

A guide line is any physical feature that can be used by a blind traveller to locate any particular object, as in the illustration where the girl is 'trailing' the door to locate the knob. A guide line can be a wall, the kerb or any change of surface along with the line of progress — e.g. the flower border in the illustration. Although the Long Cane allows its user to walk freely in the middle of the pavement, there are occasions when the cane needs to be used against a guide line: when seeking to locate a door or gate in a wall, for example. When a guide line is used the cane will make contact with it on one side and on the other side touch the ground in the normal way. The basic principle of keeping the feet and cane in opposition to each other must still be followed.

Cane – Indoor Hold

There are some situations where it is impossible to swing the cane properly, as in a busy shop or a crowded street, yet the cane can still be used to protect the body. The first method that is effective is for the subject to hold the cane vertical with the pen-holder grip in the same position as is used when ascending stairs (see illustration). The cane is swung with its tip just clearing the ground; the arc of the swing must not be wider than the shoulders. This method of travel is very useful in any crowded thoroughfare. Many congenitally blind children find it easier to learn than the second method, where the cane is held diagonally. In this method the grip is changed; the hand is slipped inwards around the cane; the thumb is straightened down the grip with the fingers curled around it (see illustration). The arm should be held forward but not rigid and the cane will stretch from a point just in front of the left foot (but not touching the ground) diagonally upwards to a point in line with the right shoulder. This, of course, applies to a right-handed user; it would be the opposite way round for a left-handed person.

CHAPTER 6

A Formal Mobility Syllabus for Children

Formal mobility is mobility activity carried on outside the precincts of the school or home. It entails a planned programme involving the use of an aid. The environments will vary widely; in a town they will range from quiet suburban streets to a busy town centre; in more rural areas the streets will tend to be much quieter but also less predictable. The nature of the particular environment is conveyed to the blind pupil through maps of different types.

Mobility lessons for congenitally blind children have a two-fold function. The programme teaches them first how to explore and appreciate a wide environment and, secondly, how to travel independently. These two facets of mobility training for children condition the curriculum so that it is somewhat different from the curriculum for the adult adventitiously blind. With adults, the primary function is to teach them to travel independently, therefore all the lessons are directed towards this aim and the widening areas in which the student travels are a reflection of his progress. A blind adult, for example, will only be given lessons at a railway station as preparation for making a journey by train on his own; these lessons will consequently come late in his training. For children who have never had sight (or very little) there is a great deal to learn about a railway station; it must be explored and appreciated in some detail. Thus the station may be visited intermittently as a 'wet day' activity. Many such children do make independent journeys by train; but even if they never reach this level they can still learn to appreciate the layout of a station and acquire the ability to move from platform to platform, and board and leave trains without physical assistance.

The syllabus that follows was developed by the author and is meant as an example of how different techniques can be gradually fitted in. It cannot be followed explicity by everybody as each syllabus must be built around the particular area where the teaching takes place. In the US for example, towns are usually built on a grid system and so mobility teachers use the 'block' as the basic unit on which to build. Again, some areas have very few pavements so it would be unrealistic to start mobility training by focusing on pavement use. The general principle to be followed is to start with the familiar environment using the appropriate teaching techniques and then to proceed to more complex and unfamiliar surroundings.

Exploring a Road Pattern

Simple Roads

The first outside lessons of the mobility syllabus should take place in what can be designated as simple roads — roads without intersections. The child should be taken round a corner of the road to be studied and line himself up against the inner shore line which is the inner boundary of the path. He should then use a Braille compass to ascertain which way the road is running. It is helpful if the first road chosen runs either directly north and south or east and west. Then he should walk up the road exploring the following features:

(1) Type of inner shore line.
(2) Type of outer shore line (this is the boundary of the outer side of the path).
(3) The general width of the path (narrow or wide) and the additional width of any verge that may exist.
(4) The surface of the path, e.g. paving stones or tarmac.
(5) The child's relationship to any traffic sounds coming from another road: the road being explored may lead off from a major road where he should be conscious of the traffic behind him.
(6) Any special feature in the fairway like a line of trees. Sometimes the child's accounts of these features can be communicated directly to the teacher; sometimes he can be asked to record them.

When the child reaches the end of the road he assumes the sighted guide position with the teacher and, together, they explore the junction made with the next road; this can be a T-junction, crossroads or a cul-de-sac. Maintaining the sighted guide position the child returns to the side of the road he has just walked up.

It is at this stage he learns how to cross a road. He begins by lining up with the kerb, crossing the road when he is satisfied it is clear of traffic. On reaching the far kerb, he swings his cane in an arc on the surface of the pavement to make sure it is clear of all obstructions. He then steps on to the pavement, moves to the inner shore line and turns to face down the road. He is then asked which direction he thinks he is facing and directed to check his judgement by using his compass. Once again he walks down the road noting the six features already listed above and checking any differences to those obtaining on the opposite pavement. When he reaches the junction he adopts the sighted guide position as before in order to explore the new road set-up. The lesson should finish with the subject recrossing the road and repeating his journey up the road but this time keeping a mid-path position. The teacher should check that he maintains a good speed, with help if necessary, and that he walks in step.

In subsequent lessons different 'simple roads' should be explored with slightly different features. A crescent road might be chosen, for example, where the child must take frequent compass bearings to check his line of direction. The child will learn another technique when he is asked to turn the corner of a road when it forms a junction, and walk a few yards down the new road. After that he retraces his steps until his cane goes over the kerb of the original road. He should practise his technique of following the kerb as a boundary until he is sure that it has straightened out from the corner; then he should line himself up to cross the road in the manner already taught.

Complex Roads

Complex roads involve intersections. In order to deal with the additional problems created by intersections the child must learn to stop when his cane detects a kerb and he must learn the new technique of *'indenting'*.

This is the practice of turning the corner into a side road before crossing it (see diagram). It ensures that the traveller does not veer into the main road. Indenting side roads is a technique which the blind person must use when he is walking along an unfamiliar route or when he is walking in an area where the corners of the roads have very rounded kerbs. Such kerbs make it difficult for him to square off in preparation to crossing the road; he may be misled and veer into the main road.

When the traveller's cane touches the kerb he turns so that he is facing the side road and walks in this direction using the kerb as a guide line. If the kerb is rounded,

INDENTING

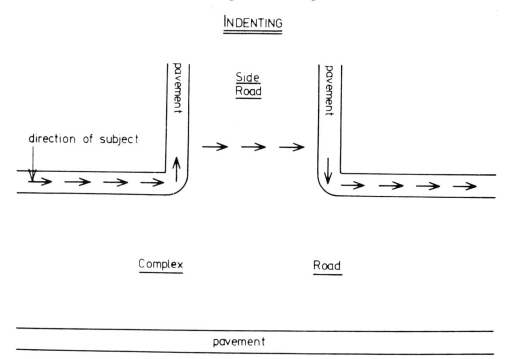

Complex   Road

pavement

he continues until it becomes parallel to him; often he may only have to walk a few steps. However, while the subject is proceeding round the corner the cane should touch the top edge of the kerb on one side of the arc and the correct swing be maintained, otherwise the traveller will be exposed to the danger of bumping into a lamp-post. Children need a lot of practice in developing this technique. One exercise that ensures that they become aware of the shape of a corner is for them to follow it using the kerb edge as a guide line. The child will start at the edge of the pavement well before the corner and, using the kerb as a guide line, walk on until he feels that he has turned the corner and the kerb is straight.

Before actually making a map of a complex road, the child will need to have had plenty of opportunity of exploring different types. The stage will be reached when one complex road will be studied in detail and a map made of it on a metal board with strips of magnetic rubber representing each road. This exercise will help a congenitally blind child to understand the layout of such a road and the junctions formed by other roads intersecting it.

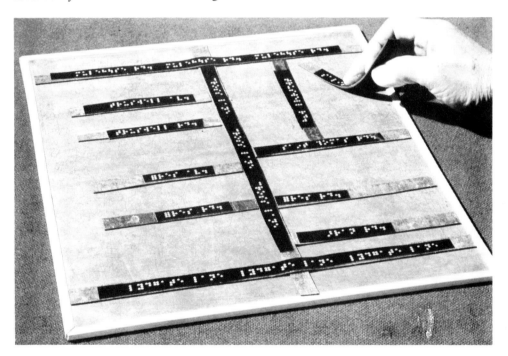

A particular local road layout may offer a good training ground in this procedure; the following example is drawn from our work in Sheffield. The road (Cross Lane — see illustration) has been especially chosen for its variety of road junctions. It runs from north to south and at both extremities joins another complex road each of which runs directly east to west. On the west side of Cross Lane itself, there are four intersections. On the east side there are three and of these one forms a cross-road over Cross Lane with the turning on the west side, another forms an 'off set' crossroad, and the third one a T-junction. Each strip of magnetic rubber representing a road has the road-name brailled on to it using Vito embossing foil. The magnetic strips of rubber that represent Cross Lane and the roads that it joins at its north and south extremities are longer than the rubber strips representing the side turnings; thus the map can be extended later.

The child starts at the south end of Cross Lane on the west pavement. He fixes his position by compass and then puts the strip of rubber representing Cross Lane in the correct position on the magnetic board. He walks along the west pavement in a northward direction until he comes to the first side road when he is given the board on which he places the named representation of this side road. Before crossing the road, the inner shore line of the corner is examined and identified as the north-west corner by a castellated wall which will enable him to identify the corner again. Having indented and crossed the road he examines the far corner in a similar manner. He then records on a portable tape-recorder the name of the road and the clues by which it can be identified. The walk is continued northwards along Cross Lane repeating the above exercise at every side road that is met. On reaching the northern extremity of the road the junction is explored and the complex road that crosses it is also placed on the map. The return journey is made on the east pavement. On this walk, when the child comes to a junction he crosses to the west side of Cross Lane to see which road is opposite before inserting his new side road on the map. If there is not a road opposite he will walk to the nearest junction before returning to the east pavement and placing the representation of the side road on the map.

The child can reconstruct the map at school with the aid of the tape that he has made. He can practice following the map with his index finger and work out which way he would have to turn if he wished to enter any particular side road. Some children have difficulty in doing this and it is important that this problem is overcome before more complicated maps are used. By using the small magnetic doll, described earlier in exploring a room, the child can be shown, for example, that when travelling north the doll moves away from him, and when turning west the doll will have to make a left turn. When the doll is travelling southwards in order to turn west the doll will have to make a right turn.

The Block

The child is next introduced to a road-pattern that encloses a block. The first blocks to be explored can be those that extend from the complex road previously studied. These can be added to the magnetic board map. This enables the child to start from a known point and he will have already explored two of the corners of the block and walked one side. When travelling around the block the child is encouraged to decide the relative lengths forming the block and its consequent shape. Having completed the block travelling in one direction the exercise is repeated the opposite way; if the directional terms clockwise and anti-clockwise are used this adds a spatial dimension to the exercise.

Recessed Maps

The next part of the programme involves a study of a map of a section of the suburbs. It is made by projecting a tracing of a 'Geographia' map on to the wall using an overhead projector. The section required is traced and the tracing laid on a sheet of magnetic rubber and cut out so that the roads may be lifted out in one piece. The latter is then put on a Thermoform machine in the reverse position so preventing the creation of a mirror-image replica; it is the recessed replica that is used for the map. Each child should have a copy of the map of the area that he is exploring; he should keep it and refer to it whenever necessary. Every map produced this way will depict the roads with sharp indentations which are smooth to the touch while the raised spaces in between retain a much rougher texture. The child should start his study of maps using this particular production; he will find it much easier to follow than a string map.

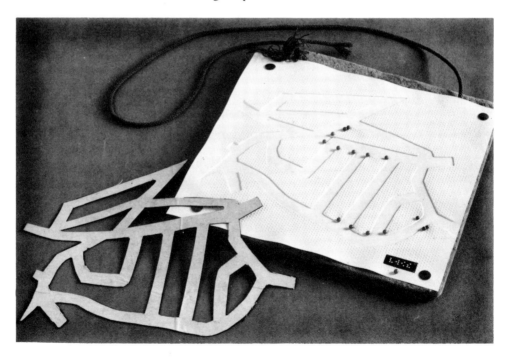

The child should begin the exercise by exploring the map with his fingers. First he is taught to identify the crescent road. This is easily recognisable by its shape and therefore makes a good point of reference. The child will already have encountered this road when it was used as an example of a simple road. In my example, the south end of the above road joins the main Manchester Road which the child next locates on the map. When he comes to walk the roads that are represented on the map, he will discover that the main road is easily discernible from other roads by two features: first the sound of the constant stream of traffic moving along and, secondly, the pavement being separated from the road by a wide grass verge with another grass verge on the inner shore line. This arrangement of grass verges is peculiar to this section of Manchester Road only. Before the child sets out on a field exercise, the map is pinned to a square of soft board with a piece of cord attached so that he can carry the map like a satchel. The first part of his training is restricted to this pattern of roads. The child walks along one of the roads represented on the map on the north side of Manchester Road. At each corner that he comes to, he marks the corresponding corner on the map with a mapping pin. When the end of the road is reached the child will find that he has marked a line of pins which depicts his route. By retracing the route and taking out the pins as he reaches each corner the child will get back to the place where he first began.

A more complicated route on the map is then pinned out on the board that will involve the subject in making different turns during his exercise. The route is discussed with the child before setting out. He is asked, for example, which way he will have to turn to get from one pin point to another. The words most used to cover the options that may be taken at corners are as follows:

(1) *Cross.* When this is written or memorised it can be shortened to C.
(2) *Left turn.* Written as L.
(3) *Right turn.* Written as R.
(4) *Cross and turn left.* Written as P. (port).
(5) *Cross and turn right.* Written as S. (starboard).

These terms were introduced at the Nottingham University Blind Mobility Research Unit. Another useful suggestion from the same source refers to the correct point at which a side road should be crossed if the subject must cross the road in order to make an opposite turn at the other end of the road (see diagram). They advise that the road should be crossed when it is first encountered rather than the subject making a simple turn and crossing the road at the other end. Obviously, therefore, the return journey along this route will differ from the outward journey.

Having practised travelling along routes on the northern section of the map made by the teacher, the child begins to pin-point his own routes. The teacher will insert two pins into the map one indicating where the route starts and the second showing where the route must finish. The child will be asked to insert pins to show how he plans to get from start to finish. He then walks the planned route.

When the child is able to walk fairly competently, the teacher should leave him a short distance from a corner to walk alone without being followed. An able pupil

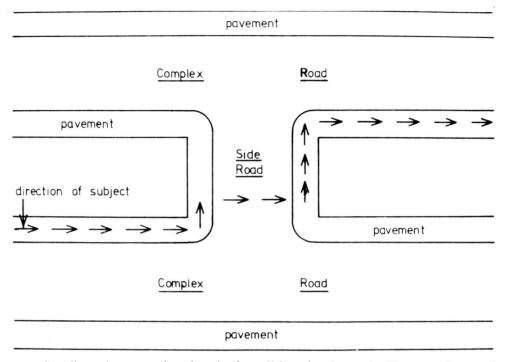

may be allowed to go solo when he is walking simple roads. The experience of feeling alone is quite an ordeal for any child and is best encountered early in his training and for a very short walk. As the child gets more sure of himself he can be told that the teacher will be at each junction and will only call out to him if it can be seen that he is in difficulties.

Finding Places on the Route: Using Clues

Using clues to find particular places along the route involves the use of echo-location. Children enjoy counting the stationary cars parked in a road and, although this exercise cannot be used as a permanent means of identifying a house, it provides a useful exercise in echo-location. To decide on a house, a number is picked at random and with the aid of the teacher it is located. The child and the teacher then return to the corner of the road from which they started and the walk to the house is repeated, all the time discovering different clues to help pin-point the house. For example, a child may need to count the number of driveways he passes before reaching the gateway of the house, identifying them by sound. Again, there may be a telegraph pole or a change of surface on the ground which will provide a clue by which the child can relate his position to the house. Practice in the application and use of clues must go on continuously.

There are obviously different routes a child can take to reach a particular point from the end of the map. This affords the opportunity of inviting the child to make a verbal map on a tape-recorder . When he exchanges his tape with a similar one made by another pupil they will both find out how explicit, or otherwise, were the instructions! When this first verbal map is made the child can be encouraged to record on the tape additional information besides the simple directional terms. He may say, for example, 'Instruction 3. Turn Left. You should now hear the sound of main road traffic in front of you.' He continues by recording the final instructions which will state the point he has reached and the tactile clues in making the location. This will give him practice in making tapes he may wish to keep for future reference and ensure that they are specific enough for him to follow perhaps a year later.

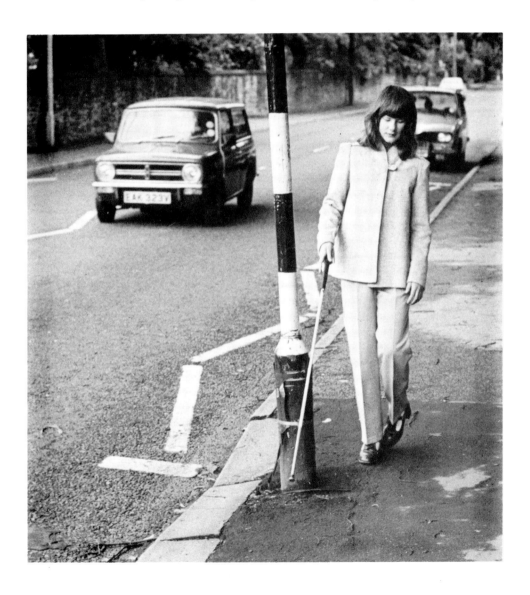

Pedestrian Crossings

The next feature on the map to which the child is introduced is a pedestrian crossing. This exercise will enable him to cross main roads and explore larger environments like the shopping precinct which is discussed below. In order to traverse a pedestrian crossing the subject must know its precise location. It can be represented on a map symbolically by two embossed parallel lines across the road, but its exact location, in reality, can only be located by identifying relevant clues. The child can be taught to find a crossing by counting a set number of strides after a particular side road or a known driveway. He then reaches the point where he must walk diagonally to the outer shore line using the latter as a guide until his cane touches the post that marks the crossing. Then he turns to face the road making sure the post is on his right-hand side; he moves a couple of paces sideways to bring him to the centre of the crossing and squares off.

The child should first listen to the near-side traffic which will (in the UK) be approaching from his right and when it is clear or he hears the driver of a car apply his brakes, he should step onto the crossing making a definite forward movement with his cane. He can then start to cross the road listening for traffic on the left-hand side. He should walk with a steady pace but be prepared to stop if necessary, should he hear a car travelling towards him on the left-hand side. On reaching the far side he must go through the drill of swinging his cane in an arc on the ground before stepping onto the kerb. If the crossing is controlled by manually-operated traffic lights, he presses the button before turning to face the road and making sure the post is on his right-hand side; again he should move a couple of paces sideways to bring him to the centre of the crossing, square off, and wait for the audible signal which will tell him when to cross.

The Shopping Area

In the area covered by the map there are shops on both sides of the road and another pedestrian crossing which will make it possible to explore both sides of the road. The map the child is using does not show the layout of the shopping area in detail so an additional map is introduced. The new map indicates the pavements, the shops, pedestrian crossing and bus stops. The child learns to find specific shops on both sides of the road, like the Post Office, the greengrocer, the chemist and a small supermarket. The expedition begins from a specific house so that it approximates to the shopping the child can do from his own home. The child actually goes shopping complete with a basket and money and makes purchases for himself and other members of the school community. The area is likely to be crowded at times and the child must adjust the cane to narrow the swing of the arc. It is possible that he may bump into other road-users particularly those looking into shop windows. He is therefore taught to stop immediately he touches anyone, bringing his cane quickly back to himself. He is encouraged to listen for other road-users, as for example the approach of a perambulator, when he is instructed to stop, then move towards the inner shore line of the pavement. A group of people standing together and talking provide an audible clue by which the child can take avoiding action.

Bus Travel

When the child is familiar with the area depicted on the shopping area map it is interesting for him to travel from school to this area by bus. Unfortunately, congenitally blind children do not have a clear concept of a bus as their experience of it is confined to getting on, sitting down and being helped off at the end of a journey. There is no time to explore a bus when it is travelling in service. At Tapton Mount School in Sheffield, there is an ex-service bus in the grounds which the children use as a play area. They are able to climb into the driver's seat and explore both decks of the bus and practise getting on and off. Nevertheless, they have to learn more about the procedure of actual bus travel. To achieve this, a service bus is brought regularly to school for the exclusive use of the children during a morning period. This ensures that there is plenty of time for the general procedure of bus travel to be practised at a leisurely pace and repeated when necessary. This is a group lesson. The children line up as they would at a bus stop. The bus is already drawn up at the roadside and the first step is to board the bus. They listen to the front door of the bus opening and move towards it trailing the side of the bus if necessary. Each of them asks for a ticket stating his intended destination and asking the driver to call out his stop; then he moves down the bus and finds a seat. No one is allowed to use the top deck; a blind person causes delay to other passengers if he attempts this feat when travelling and, furthermore, he is unable to check the stage he has reached in his journey and could easily be carried on past his stop.

The next stage is for the children to listen to the exit door when the driver opens it by remote control; each child fixes the position of the door in relation to himself. The bell for stopping the bus is also located and can be pressed by a child. When the bus stops all the children dismount and leave the bus using their canes to help them negotiate the bus step and make contact with the pavement before they step down.

This procedure is repeated several times. Eventually the bus takes the children on a regular service route. During this journey the children are told to feel distinctive bends in the road. The bus will make two stops (in fact actual request stops), and the children are reminded that this is the occasion when they must fix their positions in relation to the exit door. A little later they are told that there will be a definite turn left just before the stop where they are getting off. They must try to anticipate this stop and one child must ring the bell. Arriving, the children disembark, when they will find that they are at a bus stop which they have previously explored. They are then escorted across the road to the return bus stop using the sighted guide technique. Meanwhile the bus has made a detour in order to return to pick them up and take them to the nearest bus stop to school.

After this, bus travel on normal service routes is included in their individual lessons. At first a teacher accompanies them on the bus sitting some way behind. But when they are competent they are allowed to travel alone, being met at the end of their journey. Further progression comes later when they are met at a given place some distance away from the bus stop. Later the routes taken can involve a change of buses and finally the bus journey may be, in some cases, the means by which a child goes home alone where, at first, he would be met by his parents.

Further Routes

The child is now introduced to embossed maps of other areas of the town. The maps for these have been traced from an Ordnance Survey Map with a scale of 12:2,500 which is a slightly smaller scale than that used for the first indented map. The construction of such maps is described in *The Teaching of Science and Mathematics to the Blind* (see further reading list). The roads are depicted by raised lines, single or double. Double lines are used more frequently as a route can be pinned out on them in the same way as in an indented map. Symbols representing crossings, bus stops and buildings can be put on these maps. The routes are chosen in order to teach the child how to negotiate specific places but, by using the map, the child can also

appreciate how each route relates to the neighbourhood. The route, for example, to the shops in which the school is situated not only teaches the child where the shops and bus stops are in relation to the school but also directs him to cross a fairly busy road unprotected by a pedestrian crossing. In taking this route the child must practise obtaining sighted help in the way described earlier.

A specific route on another map will then be taken which involves a child crossing at a traffic light. He is instructed to make such crossings only if he is travelling in a known area. Some traffic lights are 'off set' and are too hazardous for him or any blind person to cross without sighted help. There is, however, a technique which a competent blind traveller can use at traffic lights with which he is familiar and this is taught to the more able pupil. The blind person should square up in the same manner as when traversing a pedestrian crossing. He must listen to one complete change of the lights and then cross the road at the moment he hears the traffic starting up parallel to the direction he must take to move over the crossing.

Maps for the Blind

One of the problems encountered in making an effective map for the blind person is that the map is very difficult to read if it carries too much information. Maps must always be simple even if it proves necessary to provide several maps of the same area each showing different data. In order to achieve this in the maps for children, it is possible to use an 'overlay system'. Two sheets of 'Rayophane' paper are attached by ringed binders on each side of the raised map so that each sheet can fold over it (see photograph). The names of the roads are brailled on the Rayophane sheets using Vito embossing foil. The roads that run more or less vertically are put on one of the attached sheets and the remaining roads on the other so that the names overlay the appropriate roads on the centre map. The child is able to identify any road by reference to the relevant overlay. He can pick out roads and mark routes by fixing pins under the 'Rayophane' sheets on the main map.

Another useful method of mapping a route or illustrating such features as a road junction or underpass is by recording these on a *Dunwell Frame*. This consists of a rubber pad centred on a piece of hardboard over which a stout cardboard frame fits tightly. The base and frame are bound together along one side to form a hinge like a book binding. The map is made by placing a piece of Rayophane paper over the rubber pad base and clamping it down with a cardboard frame (see illustration). Diagrams and routes can be embossed on the paper using a ball-point pen. The tracings can be taken from a map or drawn freehand.

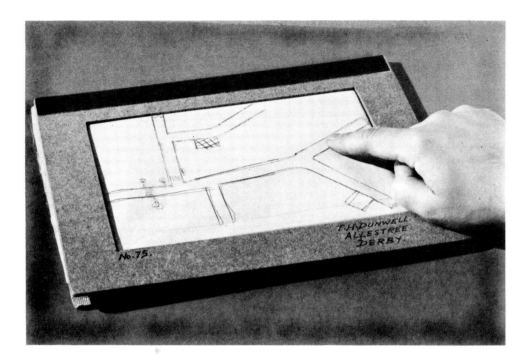

Tape Maps

Routes that are sufficiently interesting for the child to wish to keep details of them
may be recorded on a small cassette by the child himself. Phillips have produced a
very useful pocket tape-recorder especially adapted for the blind. The user is able to
record a set number of 'bleeps' at the end of each route; these signals are heard as the
tape is rewound and serve to act as a form of index. The child should keep a record in
a Braille note-book in which he writes the name of each route and the number of
bleeps that precede it.

Advanced pupils can use tape maps to record routes to specific places in town.
Each route should start by recording the location of the bus stop and the number of
the bus needed. Many of these routes are to places which have already been
explored in isolation such as the railway station, a large underpass, the library, the
theatre and large departmental stores. The child will eventually become so
competent that he will be able to find his way through busy streets and make
journeys that will involve taking two buses.

The final part of the mobility syllabus concentrates on the way a child conducts
himself whilst travelling rather than just getting from one place to another. For
example he is taken to a coffee shop in the centre of the town: he begins by finding
his way to the counter, under instruction, buys the coffee and finds a free table.
When he attempts to do all this on his own he will have some difficulty finding a free
table and he will minimise this problem, particularly for other people, if he asks the

assistant politely if she will show him to a free table. By using the public in such a way the blind person does not lose his independence but gains the respect of the sighted world.

Mobility for Partially Sighted Children

The training described in this syllabus outline has been primarily concerned with children whose vision is either non-existent or so reduced that they are unable to perceive the outlines of objects. The term 'visually handicapped' in fact covers a wide spectrum of visual impairment and includes a large group of children whose vision cannot be relied upon to enable them to travel freely in all types of environment without the assistance of some mobility training. This is why systematic instruction must be given to children within this group.

First, they should be equipped with any low visual aid that will benefit them. Many children, for instance, can be helped to see more clearly if they are equipped with a small monocular aid which will enable them to see the numbers on buses and the names of streets; a hand-held magnifier will help them to verify the contents of a packet and to read the price tag when shopping in a supermarket. Secondly, all visually handicapped people should carry a folding cane that they can use when necessary. The type of cane used will vary according to the immediate needs of the individual. A short folding cane is useful in a busy street; people coming towards a visually handicapped person who is carrying a cane will take avoiding action and so leave him a clear path. Some will have difficulty in locating the exact position of steps and kerbs; for them longer folding canes that will reach to the ground are of great benefit. Crossing busy roads can be quite hazardous for this group and, again, a cane held diagonally across the body when standing at the kerb will signify that assistance is needed.

Quite clearly, the mobility scheme of any school for the visually handicapped must include a programme for partially sighted children. The research of Barraga in the 1960s and that of Tobin, Tooze and Chapman in the 1970s has shown that training in the use of residual vision improves the subject's visual perception. In mobility, this training takes the form of teaching the child to look for visual as well as tactile clues.

Map training for this group is an excellent means of teaching them to perceive the larger environment. Map work can begin with the child constructing a map on the magnetic board with strips of rubber of the road described earlier in this chapter. However, the partially sighted child will construct both sides of the road simultaneously instead of exploring each side separately. This will encourage him to look beyond his immediate surroundings. During this exercise he will be able to learn to cross roads safely using the same drill already outlined for blind subjects but with the additional advantage of being able to look both ways for approaching cars.

Raised maps of areas can be made easier for the child with residual vision to see by marking over the embossed lines with a black felt-tip pen. Routes can be pinpointed on the map in the same way as for totally blind children but the partially sighted child will discover additional clues visually. Shopping areas, for example, may be explored and relevant street furniture noted like the post box that indicates a post office. Partially sighted children are further encouraged to find dominant visual clues by which they can orientate themselves. An excellent exercise for the partially sighted child is for him to be told that he will have to retrace the route he is walking exactly. It will stimulate him to take note of visual clues so that he can help himself by identifying them on his return journey. All aspects of travel techniques are practised until the child feels sufficiently competent to walk alone and use various kinds of public transport.

Children who have a degenerative condition of the eye or suffer from night blindness should be given practice in travelling under a blindfold using a Long Cane. Most children enjoy this experience if it is structured systematically for short spells at a time. It is a useful preparation for them when their sight does finally go; travelling without the aid of sight is then not new to them.

Mobility lessons should be enjoyable to the children and different teaching techniques should be devised to maintain a sense of adventure and discovery. However limited children's natural abilities are, all of them can improve with practice. Above all, they will achieve a greater measure of independence and their lives will be correspondingly enriched. One of Bilbo's poems from Tolkein's *Lord of the Rings* seems most apposite.

The Road goes ever on and on
Down from the door where it began.
Now far ahead the Road has gone
And I must follow, if I can.

They can!

Recommended Further Reading

Cratty, B.J. (1971) *Movement and Spatial Awareness in Blind Children and Youth* (Springfield, Illinois: Charles C. Thomas)

Chapman, E.K. (1978) *Visually Handicapped Children and Young People* (London: Routledge and Kegan Paul)

Lowenfeld, B. (ed.) (1973) *Our Blind Children* (Springfield, Illinois: Charles C. Thomas)

RNIB (1968) *The Teaching of Science and Mathematics to the Blind* (London: RNIB)

Tobin, M.J., Tooze, F. and Chapman, E.K. (1979) *Look and Think* (London: RNIB)

About the Author

Together with her husband Freddie, formerly Headmaster of Tapton Mount School, Sheffield, Doris Tooze has done pioneering work in the area of mobility training for visually handicapped children. Her achievements have received national and international recognition and she regularly lectures on courses organised by the International Council for the Education of the Visually Handicapped and held all over the world. Apart from her practical work she has conducted research into the differences in spatial awareness between congenitally and adventitiously blind children. Her present book is, therefore, the outcome of wide-ranging experience and detailed knowledge, almost unique of its kind.

Index